SUNSPOT

SUNSPOT

The Best Ever Astrological Guide to Your Dog

by Laurie Birnsteel

CUMBERLAND HOUSE
Nashville, Tennessee

Published by
    CUMBERLAND HOUSE PUBLISHING, INC.
    431 Harding Industrial Drive
    Nashville, Tennessee 37211
    www.cumberlandhouse.com

Cover design by Unlikely Suburban Design, Nashville, Tennessee.

Library of Congress Cataloging-in-Publication Data

Birnsteel, Laurie, 1946–
    Sunspot : the best ever astrological guide to your dog / Laurie Birnsteel.
        p. cm.
    ISBN 1-58182-264-2 (alk. paper)
    1. Astrology and pets. 2. Dogs—Miscellanea. I. Title.
BF1728.3.B57 2002
133.5'86367—dc21

                                                                    2002002002

Printed in the United States of America

1 2 3 4 5 6 7 8 9 10—06 05 04 03 02

CONTENTS

INTRODUCTION

A friend and I were discussing our dogs when she said, "My dog hates change. If I put a new tag on him, he pouts for days."

"Was your dog born in May?" I asked.

She said yes.

"Well, there you go! Your dog's a Taurus and Tauruses hate change."

Later, I started thinking about our conversation. The last dog who owned me was a Gemini, and I never knew if she would lift her leg or squat. Like the zodiac twins, she had different and distinct personalities. She could be sweet with someone one minute and growl at them the next. I chalked it up to her being weaned too early. But the more I thought about dogs and their astrological signs, the more I wondered if there were a connection. Lili, the dog who owns me now, is a Cancer. She's gentle, not confrontational, emotional, and melodramatic. I'm also a Cancer and possess similar traits. Does Lili act as I do because she's my dog or because we share the same sign?

Curious, I visited local bookstores to see if there were anything written on dog or animal astrology. I found nothing. I scanned Amazon.com and Barnesandnoble.com on the Internet and there, to my chagrin, found a number of books on the subject. My idea was not new; it had been pawed and penned more than once. However, most of the books were written in the '70s when Linda Goodman's classic *Sun Signs* appeared. (Remember those days when "What's your sign?" seemed to be the first question asked when meeting someone new?) I decided not to read what had already been written. If I were to tackle the subject, it was going to be my own interpretation. I didn't want to be influenced by what others had to say.

Although I am not a professional, I do believe in astrology. Having studied the subject, I felt secure enough in my understanding to embark on this project. I started talking to any dog owners I met about their dog's personality. When I told them I was writing a book on dog astrology, the reaction was overwhelming, their enthusiasm infectious. Everyone thought it was a great idea, and not one person rolled their eyes while twirling their index finger in that "she's crazy" gesture of accusation when I told them my plans. At least not to my face.

I created a questionnaire for each sun sign. Having an intuitive knowledge of children, I kept them in mind when applying human characteristics to the kingdom of canines. (Let's face it, our dogs are our kids.) Next, I started passing out the questionnaires to friends. Word spread. A reporter heard about me and set up an interview. The story appeared in the *Courier-Journal,* Louisville's local newspaper. In a matter of days, I received hundreds of phone calls from people wanting their dogs included in my research. I mailed the questionnaires to everyone who contacted me. It wasn't long before I was on the radio telling listeners about my project. With my permission, a television crew filmed a segment for their nightly news magazine. A local cable station called and I appeared on their show about pets. Meanwhile, the number of responses continued to grow. What began as a simple conversation had turned into quite an undertaking. When another disc jockey asked me to do a one-hour segment on his Saturday afternoon call-in program, I said no. I realized enough was enough. I needed to put pen to paper if I were ever to start, much less finish, this book.

Sun Spot: The Best Ever Astrological Guide To Your Dog has been a hoot to write. I want to thank everyone, all my old and new friends, for participating.

My appreciation also extends to Wilma Crisler and Nolan Myers, professional astrologers, who were always there to answer my questions. I also want to give a big hug to Holly Onachilla, my dog-walking friend. It was Holly who suggested the title of this book. Finally, I want to thank my editor, Hope Hollenbeck, who made this book readable.

TAIL END

My dog-walking friend Marie told me this story and I think it's appropriate here. When Marie's son was about nine, he came home after spending the night with a friend.

"Oh, Mom," he said. "They have the cutest puppy I've ever seen!"

"What kind is it?" Marie asked.

He thought a moment, then said, "I don't know. It's a cross between two breeds."

A few more moments passed. Suddenly, he said, "I know. I remember now, it's a Cockashitz!"

Cockapoo or Cockashitz, I hope that's not what you'll think after reading *Sun Spot: The Best Ever Astrological Guide To Your Dog.*

AUTHOR'S NOTES

Or
A Little More Information
You May Or May Not Want To Know

Within astrology, there are 12 basic personalities, each based on the characteristics of the sign of the month of birth.

HOUSES

An astrological chart looks like a wheel divided into 12 equal wedges. Each wedge, which represents a sun sign, is also referred to as a house. In simple terms, house is like one's home; it is a place of comfort, a place where one's relationship to the world is defined. Each house has a motto, or words, which reflect the feelings of that particular house. For example; Aries is the first house in the zodiac. It's motto is "I am" (number one). The word best used to describe this house is ego.

SYMBOLS

Each of the twelve constellations in astrology is symbolized by the image depicted in the formation of its stars. For example, in Aries the stars form the Ram, Cancer's show The Crab, Libra's image form The Scale. You'll find that words that are associated with each symbol will help describe characteristics of that sun sign. Rams can be rambunctious, Crabs clingy, and Bulls stubborn.

PLANETS

Each constellation/sun sign has a ruling planet and each planet represents a motivation. Planets influence the way a particular house relates to the world. In this book I discuss Venus and its influence on Libra because it helps in understanding the Libra personality. Because planets aren't stationary and their elliptical paths differ, no one's chart is the same. Also, planetary placement depends on the exact time and place of birth, something one would most likely not know about his or her pet.

QUALITIES

As a layman, I find this term deceptive as are the three terms used to define qualities; cardinal, fixed and mutable. The easiest way to explain what qualities are is by using the words beginning, middle, and end. Qualities are based on the placement of one's sun sign and its position in its season. Cardinal signs begin a season, fixed signs are the middle months, and mutable signs mark the end of a season's cycle. Cardinal signs initiate change and are restless, while fixed signs tend to be set in their ways. Mutable signs, although they don't initiate change, live in anticipation of that change. They're easily bored if nothing is happening. Simplified visually:

	Cardinal	Fixed	Mutable
Spring	Aries	Taurus	Gemini
Summer	Cancer	Leo	Virgo
Fall	Libra	Scorpio	Sagittarius
Winter	Capricorn	Aquarius	Pisces

THE CUSP

The cusp is the transition point, the dividing line between one sun sign and the next. If one is born on the first three days of a sun sign or the last three days of a sun sign, one is on the cusp. For example, I was born on July 22, which is on the cusp between Cancer and Leo. I am what astrologers refer to as a Late Cancer.

If your birthday is on a cusp, I suggest reading both horoscopes. For example, I can combine some of my Cancer characteristics with those of Leo. If I were born on June 24, I'd be called an Early Cancer and would look for the Gemini traits I might possess. Personally, I've always found the characteristics to be within the demarcation dates used by the majority of astrologers. Yes, sometimes I may act like a Leo, but I'm a Cancer through and through.

THE ELEMENTS

Each of the twelve signs of the zodiac are divided into four elements: Earth, Air, Fire, and Water. Each of these elements reflects the emotional and personality aspect of its sun sign. Many of the slang terms and cliches you've heard all your life appropriately describe the characteristics found in the four elements. The phrase "down-to-earth" describes the Earth signs. "Space cadet" works with the Air element. You know that phrase "out of one's element"? Well, now you really know what it means!

Fire Signs

Aries, Leo, and Sagittarius. Fire signs are excitable, high-spirited, exuberant, and energized. They respond to situations with an intensity and tend to be impulsive rather than rational. But remember: Flames become embers. Fire signs can also be passionate, warm, and comforting. In general, Aries is excited by adventure, Leo basks in the warmth of his domain, and Sagittarius explodes with enthusiasm.

Air Signs

Gemini, Libra, and Aquarius are sociable, expressive, diverse, and persuasive. Landing these sun signs can be difficult as they're hard to hold. Although most air signs are smart, their airwaves can differ. Geminis prefer to use their minds, and Libra their hearts, while Aquarius . . . well Aquarians live in the moment. Air signs can be gentle and breezy or tornadic! Mentally, emotionally and physically, be prepared for a fun but bumpy flight.

Earth Signs

Taurus, Virgo, and Capricorn. Solid, reserved, steady, dependable, practical, and calm. Earth signs can be stubborn and are known for their ability to "dig in." Tauruses don't like any changes to their physical environment, and security means the most to them. Virgos are perfectionists, and anything out of place will throw them into a twit. But there are also Virgos who are slobs. Capricorns likes predictability and routine.

Water Signs

Cancer, Scorpio, and Pisces. Water signs live in their feelings; emotions determine their behavior. They are Intuitive, empathetic, sympathetic, and melodramatic. Cancers' emotions are open and out front. You might say they wear their hearts on their sleeves. Scorpios' waters run deep. They are submerged in mystery and can be hard to fathom. Pisces reflect their surroundings but, like Scorpio, one's never sure what is really hidden beneath the surface.

Remember, all elements can take different shapes. They can condense, expand, solidify, or flow. If your sign and your dog's conflict, think positive. If your element is water and your dog's element is fire, combined the two make steam heat, positive energy.

The day and month your dog was born is all you need to interpret your dog's astrological sign. If you don't know its birth date, read all the chapters, then give Bowser the birthday that fits him the best. During my research, I had a call from someone who owned a stray. At the time she found him, her veterinarian thought the dog was about eight months old. I counted back ten months, and started giving her the characteristics of Aquarius and Pisces. Neither applied, but when I described a Taurus, bingo!

This also happened during the course of my research. I got a call one day from a lady who said, "I was working on your questionnaire and thought, this isn't my dog. Then I looked at the date and realized I was answering for a Capricorn. My dog's a Sagittarius!" Needless to say, I was pleased to hear that tale, particularly after her pet really fit the characteristics of a Sagittarius.

BREEDS

Every breed has its own particular characteristics. Hounds use their keen sense of smell to track animals, humans included. Sporting dogs such as pointers, setters, and retrievers point, set, or retrieve respectively. Terriers ferret prey from their dens beneath the earth's surface. Working or herding dogs are bred to do just that—work with herds. Toy dogs are little replicas of their larger counterparts. Today, these lap dogs make easy-to-care-for pets, Non-Sporting dogs, referred to as Utility dogs in England, are a potpourri of various breeds not specified by the American Kennel Club. Some dog books even refer to companion dogs, which, to me, is redundant.

Although this book isn't about breeds, you might take their heritage into consideration when thinking about their sun sign. For example, a Welsh Corgi was bred to herd. If you own a Corgi who was born an Aries, your dog will want to be the leader of the pack. However, if your Corgi was born under the sign of Cancer, his herding tactics will be more like mothering maneuvers. A thought for you to ponder.

And that's all folks . . . .

CRIES

The Ram

 GOOD DOGGY:

adventurous
confident
competitive
energetic
enthusiastic
independent
impulsive
spirited
tireless

BAD DOGGY:

arrogant
brash
brusque
excitable
impatient
impulsive
reckless
selfish

PAW PRINTS:

Emma Ayres, Jack Russell Terrier
Crystal Early, Jack Russell Terrier
Piper Gray, Nova Scotia Duck Tolling Retriever
Tillie Hancock, Labrador
Cora Heuser, West Highland White Terrier
Maybelline Jones, Labrador Retriever
Max Tucci, Yorkshire Terrier
Bunni Williams, Norwich Terrier

ARIES
March 21–April 20
The Ram
I Am

When I first embarked on this project, I spent a lot of time observing dogs in the nature preserve I frequent. One Yorkshire Terrier named Max intrigued me. He was fearless, independent, greeted all dogs great or small as if they were equal to his size, and would take to the wetlands sending ducks and geese into flight as he plunged through the swamps. One afternoon, I asked his owner when he was born.

"End of March," she said

I had suspected Max was an Aries, and the confirmation thrilled me.

The constellation ARIES, symbolized by The RAM, is the first house in the zodiac, the first month of spring, and the first sun sign with the element of FIRE. Aries represents beginnings, resurrection as it were, and change. Ablaze with the colors of spring, Aries bursts into bloom as winter's chill leaves the air.

Aries is the infant in the celestial sky, and when this baby wants his needs met, he wants his needs met *now!* Aries is the most ME oriented of the sun signs. When you think of Aries, think in terms of instant gratification.

Princess Emma is a Jack Russell Terrier and whatever Emma wants, Emma gets. Her owner wrote:

> *If we're going somewhere and I get delayed by a phone call, Emma becomes very impatient. First she'll stare at me and will start with a whisper that sounds like "poof." The longer she has to wait, the louder*

she gets. Poof becomes woof about every thirty seconds. As a last resort, Emma will bark very loudly. Deafened by decibels, I'm forced to hang up to shut her up.

Accompanying the ME FIRST attitude is Aries' motto: I AM—which translates into I am going to be the first to catch that ball, I am going to be the first dog in the car because I AM NUMBER ONE, I AM TOP DOG!

When we brought Max home, we were concerned about our three-year-old Springer Spaniel, Toffee. In fact, when I first put Max down, I was sure Toffee would take him for a $300 snack. Immediately it was clear though, that Max was a take-charge kind of dog. From that moment on, Toffee became his special responsibility.

Toffee was a quiet, gentle dog who never learned to scratch or bark to be let out. She'd just stand at the door, legs crossed metaphorically, waiting for someone to notice. Max noticed and took control. He'd run to us, bark, run to the door, bark, then run back to us. He kept this up until someone responded to Toffee's needs.

If by some chance your Aries isn't number one in the pecking order, (almost unheard of), this sun sign will turn any situation to its advantage. One Aries dog I know has three other housemates with which he shares car space. He isn't always the first to hop in, but you can bet he gets the best seat, the one directly behind the driver. That way, he can lay his head on her shoulder and get his ears rubbed as she drives.

Emma isn't always first in the car. Woody, my other Jack Russell, is a Taurus and will barrel right over anything that gets in his way. But once in the car, Emma always gets to ride on the center armrest, which is her lookout point.

Aries' icon is the RAM, and like a RAM, Aries is RAMbunctious and will not hesitate to RAMrod his way into a situation. They are headstrong and determined-determined to do things their way. If provoked, an Aries won't hesitate to lock horns with the opposition. When you think of Aries, think of Sylvester Stallone's character RAMbo.

Piper, as in The Pied Piper, is a Nova Scotia Duck Tolling Retriever. Okay, I know what you're thinking. You never heard of that breed. So I will digress here. The Nova Scotia Duck Tolling Retriever was created to toll (lure) and retrieve waterfowl. It is a blend of Golden, Chesapeake, and Flat- coated Retrievers, with a little brown Cocker Spaniel, Irish Setter, and maybe a little farm Collie thrown in. The dog resembles a red fox, which ducks will approach out of curiosity. Now, back to Piper.

Piper has always felt he was the alpha male. He has learned the hard way that sometimes he is not, but that doesn't stop him from trying to assert (ram) himself again and again against the same more dominant dogs. Piper has a very high energy level and will walk in circles waiting for a door or gate to be opened. When he comes into the field with other dogs, he's like an anarchist in the crowd, agitating the others to play or follow him into the creek.

As Piper's owner noted, Piper has a very high energy level. That's because Piper's element is fire, and you'll find words that pertain to fire describe the nature of Aries. Fire signs are energetic, eager, dynamic, enthusiastic, impulsive, spirited, and combustible. When soothed, they can become warm fuzzies.

We used to take Max to a field less than a mile away from our home. Knowing his destination, Max would ricochet between the back and front seats, barking the entire time it took to drive there. One day, he completed 47 laps during the drive between our house and the field.

Keeping up with an Aries can be a challenge because they're fearless. When asked about this, Max's owner wrote:

Max loves varmint chasing. When he was young, he was down every hole in the ground as quick as Bob's-Your-Uncle. Being so small, lots of holes were accessible to him, but larger holes certainly didn't daunt him.

We were always afraid that whatever he was pursuing would decide to fight rather than flee out its back door. Max was, if you'll pardon the pun, dogged in his pursuit and no amount of coaxing could induce him to come out from under the terrain. We could hear his muffled yelps under our feet. Sometime he'd be yards from the entrance.

Once we drove home from the field in frustration to get a shovel to dig him out. When my husband returned to the parking lot, he found a young man standing there who asked if we had lost a dog.

Well, we hadn't exactly lost him; we thought we knew where he was. But it seems Max reappeared while we were gone, and the boy's girlfriend had scooped up the lost dog and taken him home, leaving her boyfriend behind.

By the time we got to the girlfriend's house, she had bathed, combed, be-ribboned, and perfumed him. I suspect we arrived just before she would have put him in doll clothes.

If your Aries is easily distracted, be prepared to follow their circuitous route. Like the March Hare in *Alice in Wonderland,* Aries act as if they're late for a very important date! Believe me, your Aries probably has no clue as to what that date's about, but it doesn't matter. For Aries, every new experience will be a wonder and there are many wonders to experience.

> *Max always knows exactly where he wants to be—and often where he wants to be is on the road having adventures. The only one in our family with a police record is Max, who has been picked up in three municipalities. Max likes being with me, but being with me just means being in the same county.*

Aries loves the rugged life of the great outdoors. Piper will stay outside when it rains and will sleep on the deck during a non-thunderous storm. When his owner takes him to the woods, Piper moves off trail through thick bushes with no trouble. Emma, too, has been known to take off only to return with a face crusty with dirt and pond scum on her paws.

It's better to socialize Aries early. Because they want to be number one, this sun sign needs to realize he's not the only pooch on the planet. Aries will play with other dogs but will run off if distracted by something as simple as a butterfly.

> *Piper loves the company of other dogs and people, especially women. He will play by himself when alone but only for a short time. It's the same when I'm playing with him. He will retrieve for a short time. Then he'll catch the ball and not return until he's carried it several laps around the back yard.*

Aries can come across as having an attitude, which is most apparent in their stance and gait. Fire signs like to strut their stuff. Keep in mind, however, that Rams can be gentle as lambs.

> *Piper will prance and arch his long bushy tail when approaching new dogs. Piper has, on more than one occasion, ended up retreating with his tail between his legs as he runs full speed back to the house or to me.*

> *Emma has a tendency to tackle my cats, one at a time. She gets them in a headlock but then will tenderly lick their ears.*

Aries don't like taking orders, and as mentioned, they have a way of turning things to their own advantage. I'm sure you've experienced that look, the *"Me? You want me to do what?"* look. If this is their reaction, use a firm voice and eye contact to get their attention. Once you have their attention, talk to them. Aries like to know why, so explain what you want them to do and why. That's right, look your dog in the eye and tell him what you want. Then if he obeys, show your happiness. Express your joy when he sits or stays on command. Be enthusiastic and dramatic. Your dog will feel like he really is number one. But don't get too carried away. If your Aries thinks you're yelling at him, he'll cower, and you will blow the whole thing.

> *Piper learns by watching and, with repeated instruction, will catch on but only on his own terms. He failed an obedience class. The trainer said he was one of the smartest dogs he had handled and would obey once or twice to show he could do something, but after that, Piper would refuse the command. Piper is quick to learn but his attention span is short.*

On the other hand, there is Max. Max, well, Max was born to be the trainer.

From puppyhood, Max understood very quickly what we wanted him to do, but he was not very interested in doing it. Our original plan when we got Max was to give him to my husband's recently widowed mother, Nana. We thought he'd be good company and occupy her time. We kept him for a few months, occasionally dropping him off at Nana's to spend the day. In August, we moved him in with her. Right away, Max took control, and within a week, Nana called to complain. Max doesn't eat a thing.

I was suspicious. You know what an Italian grandmother's idea of "not eating a thing" means. So I questioned, Not a thing? You mean he's died of starvation?

"Well not quite," Nana replied.

Turns out Max would eat McDonald's hamburgers—but only the plain ones—not the ones all gooped up with special sauce. I asked how she found out Max liked plain hamburgers and she said, "Max has two kinds of barks. One kind means he just wants to go for a ride in the car. The other means he wants to go to McDonald's."

I have no explanation for how he communicated the meaning of his barks to her—mental telepathy, perhaps. Eventually Nana started stockpiling hamburgers in the refrigerator in case bad weather or her ill health kept her from taking him out.

Sadly, in a few years Nana became too ill to keep Max, and he returned to our home after a month's stay in the kennel, a stay made not too onerous as he charmed the staff into letting him have the run of the waiting room.

Max, Piper, and Princess Emma were three of eight Aries interviewed for this book. Other comments of owners of this sun sign were:

Energetic? Maybelline will chase a ball or swim in the pool (preferably both) from sunup to sundown. And she has to be first to catch that ball even if it means nearly drowning others in the process. She is very enthusiastic but can be a big sissy when pushed or pulled. One would think she was being flogged. When playing tug of war, she'll be the first to drop the rope and walk away. If she sees a dead bird, she sniffs it, then walks away. She's not interested in things that don't move. Maybelline loves the outdoors, is gentle, tireless, and loyal.

Bunni bounces and hops like a rabbit. You can really see her strut her stuff. She always wants to impress. When I bring her home from work, she plows right into my roommate's dog and knocks him to the ground. Late at night, though, she lies beside him and licks his ears.

When I brought a new puppy home, Cora let him know she was boss. She lets him know when she needs her space. She lets me know when she needs her space. If we get on her nerves, she simply leaves the room. Cora doesn't need a playmate. She has her daily dose of birds and squirrels to keep her happy and challenged.

Patience? What is patience? Tillie is the most gas-happy dog I've ever owned, always ready to go somewhere. I've got a lot of dogs but Tillie will manage to get the closest to me where-ever we are, in the car or on the bed. She is independent and she wants to do what she wants to do, not what I want. Tillie has great determination and succeeds in doing what she wants better than any other dog I've ever owned.

With Crystal, everything has to be now. Without a doubt, she wants to be top dog. She was easy to train because she has a great determination to succeed. Sweet talking to her works better than yelling. She is loyal, loving, and beautiful!

Not long ago, I saw Max's mom getting out of her car carrying a book. "Where's Max?" I asked.

"Somewhere in there," she said pointing toward the nature preserve. "He got so far ahead of me, I went home and got something to read."

Moral? If you own an Aries, patience will be your virtue. These are the pioneers of the Zodiac. If you can't always keep up with them, relax. They'll get back to you eventually.

TAURUS
The Bull

 GOOD DOGGY:
- dependable
- determined
- gentle
- grounded
- loyal
- mature
- patient
- practical
- reliable

BAD DOGGY:
- greedy
- inflexible
- jealous
- lazy
- stubborn
- temperamental

PAW PRINTS:

Woody Ayres, Jack Russell Terrier
Kodie Bitely, Schipperkee
Casey Bridendall, Golden Retriever
Charlie Fitzner, Maltese
Oscar Gordon, Miniature Schnauzer
Truman Harris, Shih Tzu
Maggie May Mauch, Beagle
Pisa Meador, Standard Poodle

Cady McGavic, Golden Retriever
Chardon Miller, Miniature Poodle
Frauline Mitchell, Dachshund
Callie Murphy, Shetland Sheep Dog
Doe Dog Putters, Bearded Collie
JuJu B Sikes, Jack Russell Terrier

TAURUS
April 21–May 21
The Bull
I Have

As mentioned, the first time I actually thought about dog astrology was when I heard a woman complaining:

If I change his collar, Kodie gets very withdrawn and unsocial. He hates it if I move furniture. He pouts and gives me the silent treatment.

"Was your dog born in May?" I asked.

"Yes", she replied.

Well, that explains it. Your dog is a Taurus.

TAURUS the BULL is the second house in the zodiac. Being the middle month between the beginning and end of spring, this sun sign is fixed in its ways. Taurus is the first sign with the element of Earth. Its motto is I HAVE. Whereas Aries is off discovering the world, Taurus is more interested in settling down. Like the little Spanish bull in *The Story of Ferdinand the Bull*, Tauruses would rather sit in the shade of a big old tree and smell the flowers.

Taurus is a no-nonsense dog who doesn't like conflict. He is cautious and can suffer angst if separated from the creature comforts of home. You'll find Taurus friendly but not overly demonstrative. They're more likely to come to you for a good-dog pat then mosey off to look at something else.

Tauruses are laid back and unhurried. In fact, their character is similar to that of John Wayne. They are slow and deliberate and can be described as the quintessential *Pokey Little Puppy*. Don't try to rush a Taurus as they will take their own sweet time getting from point A to point B. That's not to say this sun sign can't be impatient. When Aries want something, they become energized and fraught with urgency, but when Tauruses want something, they are persistent. After all, this Bull is just that, bull-headed and stubborn.

When we're on a walk, I often stop and talk to neighbors. Casey will sit patiently, but when she's had enough, she starts to growl viciously and bite her leash. This is her signal for me to stop talking and get going. As soon as I start to walk again, she gets quiet and wags her tail.

Chardon won't let up if she wants something. She won't stop playing, won't get off my lap, won't come in when called unless really scolded. Often I have to go outside to get her as she'll just sit there and not budge. She also won't open her mouth if I want to give her a pill or see what she's got in it!

If Oscar wants something, he gets into my lap and stares into my eyes and I can't get him to stop unless I do what he wants! Oscar will get in any car. The other day, he got into the UPS truck. He's very stubborn and won't listen. I had a heck of a time getting him out.

Kodie doesn't like getting out of bed in the morning. He growls if I try to move him. Often when I call him, he just stands there and looks like, Who me?

Pisa digs in and will not budge until she's sure of where she's being taken. She goes into a dead dog weight routine, which makes moving her next to impossible.

Callie asks for what she wants. When she doesn't get it right away, she will keep on and on and on and won't give up until it's so annoying I give in. When we're walking, she'll let me stop for awhile to talk, but when she's decided she's had enough, she grabs my slacks and pulls. She will persist until I move or get a hole in my pants leg.

Although Maggie May did well in obedience school, her stubbornness was very obvious. While she easily performed more complicated commands, she rebelled and refused to perform the basics such as sit and stay.

Taurus' element is Earth and the personality of a Taurus will be just that— grounded and down to earth. There were seventeen dogs participating in this chapter, and every owner used adjectives such as secure, patient, reliable, gentle, charming, submissive, calm, collected, basic, practical, dependable, easygoing, and loyal. Those born under the sign of Taurus seem mature even as puppies.

Nothing bothers Oscar. I think he barks only because our other dog taught him to, but I don't think he's ever really been upset. As long as he's well fed, has water, and can do what he wants when he wants, he's a happy camper.

Kodie feels as though he is human and deserving of everything. Kodie owns everything and we just borrow his stuff, like the chairs we sit in.
  My father became ill with congenital heart disease and collapsed one night. Kodie, sensing something was wrong, kept licking his face until my father regained consciousness. He helped save my dad's life.

Down-to-earth? Chardon is the only dog I've ever had that digs in dirt and mud. She even prefers to walk in mud or dirt rather than on the grass. I hate wet weather—lots of paw washing.

Putters hates baths. He loves murky water and has been rescued from muddy ponds and rivers several times.

Woody's down-to-earth all right, and sometimes underneath the earth and sometimes he has to be dug out from under the earth.

Frauline is about as close to down-to-earth you can get. Her tummy's only one inch off the floor when she walks!

Tauruses do not like change. Even the presence of someone who's come to clean your carpets or do some painting can discombobulate this sun sign. They don't get angry, they get angst. Tauruses prefer to be on solid ground. They do not like the unexpected.

A Taurus needs structure, so it's best you establish a routine early on. If you keep this in mind, along with the terms patience and stability, obedience lessons should be a snap. Once a Taurus learns something, it won't be forgotten. Since they love Mother Nature, you might want to train them outdoors.

If you're someone who moves a lot, your Taurus will need a lot of support and reassurance. It's best to try to recreate his old sleeping quarters unless he's bullied his way into your bed. If you have to board your bull, be sure he has all his favorite toys and blankets with him. A familiar article of your clothing will also help.

Casey is definitely a creature of habit. She has an internal clock that is more accurate than a Timex. She knows when it is time for her daily walk, feedings, pills, and daily car rides to retrieve children. If I'm late for any of these, Casey lets me know. If I try to tell her that the schedule has changed, she looks very puzzled. It's as if she were telling me, I know my internal clock is correct, what's with you? Quit trying to hurry me.

When I brought a new puppy home, Truman had to be put on antidepressants. He wasn't the same dog. He hates anyone intruding into his family setting.

Chardon is practical and dependable unless something changes—sounds, people, big dogs, etc. She won't perform, even though she knows what to do. . . She was a washout at obedience class. She won't stay in the room if there is a fire in the fireplace. If we drop anything or someone has headphones on for their Walkman, she'll hide in the closet.

Callie is very reluctant to try new things. I have to prod her and tell her she can do it to give her confidence. She is cautious with everything, even trying new foods. She doesn't approach people or animals, she waits for them to come to her. When she doesn't want to go somewhere, she will lie down and she's almost impossible to move . . . and she only weighs 30 pounds. When we moved, Callie wouldn't go to the bathroom into the new yard. She wouldn't even go in to the new yard. I am always having to reassure her.

Pisa has her mornings down pat. She goes out to tinkle then comes back in the house. Later, and only when she's ready, Pisa goes out for her a.m. bm. She's never done both duties in one visit. She has to be let out twice, and by no means can she be rushed!

As Woody got older and more and more trustworthy, I moved his dog bed from the kitchen to the living room where I thought he would be more comfortable. Every day when I get home from work, his bed is back in the kitchen along with his chew toys.

If I try move Oscar's bed, he jumps and tries to take it back from me.

Putters has never been the same since we moved three-and-a-half years ago. Totally disoriented! Putters hates anything unpredictable. This house has gateposts in the drive. They terrified her at first. Putter's happiest at home.

When Cady was a pup, she did not like going to dog shows. She 'protected' her own space with vicious sounding growls if any other dog walked by her cage—very improper Golden Retriever behavior! We finally stopped showing her.

I took a doll out of the closet and put it on a chair. Frauline barked so long and hard, I had to put it back in the closet. One day I changed clothes when I got home. Again, Frauline barked so long and hard my husband told me to get back into what I was wearing. My husband snores and sometimes it's so loud I sleep in the guest bedroom. Well, the first time I did that I didn't make the bed the next morning. Frau sensed something was not right and when she finally figured out what it was that was wrong, she sat and barked at the unmade bed. To this day, if I don't make that bed as soon as I get up, Frau will set to barking until I do!

Charlie loves his home territory. When he goes to visit outside of his huge fenced-in yard, he throws a fit. Many times I've tried to take him places and have had to turn back and drop him off at HIS home. He hates it if I change his regular diet. He will use his nose to dump his dish.

Those born under the sign of Taurus *love* food, any kind of food. This shows up at an early age—and a Taurus puppy is apt to be not only a *Pokey Little Puppy* but also a porky little puppy. On more than one occasion, I've heard stories—gut-wrenching stories—about a Taurus chowing down gobs of food. In fact, a dog I had years ago ate an entire taco casserole without batting an eye. Its ingredients included three pounds of ground chuck, a block of sharp Cheddar cheese, a couple of cups of Fritos, a can of kidney beans, and a cup of sour cream. This same dog also ate an entire bag of Hershey's Chocolate Kisses, foil and all. What's truly amazing is that she never got sick.

My Jack Russell ate a full pot of chili that had been placed on an outside table to cool. She was so bloated she could barely lie down; she just sort of tilted to one side, with her paws dangling at her sides. She looked like a beached blowfish.

Woody eats anything, including raiding my neighbors compost pile for bits of broccoli, brussels sprouts, carrots, or any other edible object he can get in his mouth! If I call Woody, he won't cross the threshold until I show him a dog biscuit.

When Cady was a puppy, I followed the instructions on the EuKanuba package (obviously they just want to sell puppy food). She ate five cups a day and never left a morsel. Her weight ballooned. It took a while (and a litter) to slim her down.

When Frauline was little, I had to feed her in a separate room or she'd eat the other dog's food. Frau, now three, will eat only one kind of dog food. Unfortunately, my vet says it's the kind that will make her fat.

Charlie was picky as a pup, but after the puppy stage, he ate everything and I mean everything!

Oscar will sit and shake for food, but no food, no cooperation.

Tauruses really love the outdoors, but tend to have a difficult time overcoming inertia. Like the matadors in Ferdinand the Bull, you might have to wave an imaginary cape in front of your BULL and yell olé. Better yet, oleo. He'll think you've got food and will happily follow you out the door.

Casey is practically comatose for most of the day. She becomes lively when the children come home from school. She gets her walk late in the afternoon, eats dinner, and then it's off to bed. She's awake only about 4 to 5 hours a day.

Maggie May is in no hurry to go out in the morning. She likes to sleep late and then goes out to lounge in the sun. And Maggie May is a Beagle!

Cady considers herself an indoor dog even when the others are all out. When I come home, the other dogs jump up while Caddy just lies there. When the others go out, she retreats to a corner and turns her back. After our morning walk, when the others race to the deck, Cady lags behind. If I try to force her to speed up, she puts on a poor-hurt-dog act

Frau's perfectly happy snoozing under a shade tree all day. I've had at least 12 dogs and Frau's the sleepiest of them all. She zzzz's 18 hours a day!

Pisa doesn't like it when I put her lead on, because she knows I'm going to take her for a walk. She doesn't want to go out until she is ready.

Juju-B's a couch potato who makes pillow cases into her own personal sleeping bags.

Putter sleeps so much we often think she's dead. Sleep is her favorite pastime.

Kodie loves to lounge around the house with my dad. I often find them napping together.

Tauruses like warm, physical relationships and love to be cuddled, hugged, and squeezed. Despite a tendency toward laziness, Tauruses have a great deal of strength and endurance.

Kodie runs on the treadmill, never quitting. If he tires, he will let his back paws slide onto the carpet and use only his front paws. When he gets really tired, he'll scoot from one side to the other just using one paw at a time. If I lock him out of my exercise room, he gets very hostile.

Taurus motto is I HAVE. Some of the responses I got when I asked owners to complete the sentence I HAVE were: a stubborn streak, a strong will, a positive outlook on life, a great loyalty and love for my family.

Casey is very special to our family. We almost lost her a year ago at age five when she became very ill from a twisted stomach. She had emergency surgery but became ill two months later with inflammatory bowel disease. She was in an emergency care hospital for three weeks on IVs with no food. We visited her every night and even brought children home from college to say good-bye as she was not responding to the treatment. After three weeks, the vet called to say Casey was not responding, they had done all they knew to do, and wanted to euthanize her. I understood and said okay, but I wanted to go there that night and say good-bye. My husband and my youngest daughter went with me to tell her good-bye for the last time. We hugged her, cried dearly, and then she stood up and started wagging her tail. I asked the vet what this meant, but she said she did not know as Casey had been unresponsive for weeks. I told her I didn't want her to do anything that evening. The next night when we visited, the vet told us we would be pleased. Casey had taken water by mouth without vomiting. The next day she took food and kept it down. She was home about five days later.

Our vet said he thinks our love gave Casey a reason to live. These past ten months feel like a gift to me because she is fine and acts like any other dog. I think we are all closer now and don't take Casey for granted —nor she, us. We truly love her and are grateful for whatever time we have with her.

As of this writing, Casey is alive and well. One might say that those born under the sign of Taurus have it all!

Plant your Taurus with love, and he will bloom in splendor. Just remember to be patient and don't over-fertilize!

GEMINI

The Twins

 GOOD DOGGY:
amusing
creative
communicative
curious
dualistic
expressive
versatile
vivacious
smart

BAD DOGGY:
ditzy
fickle
inconsistent
irresponsible
restless
scattered
scheming

PAW PRINTS:

 Addie Cheski, Golden Retriever
Alfie Comstock, Shih Tzu
Rush Hancock, Labrador Retriever
Agatha Hendricks, Old English Sheepdog
Georgia Heuser, Labrador Retriever
Lil Jones, German Short-hair Pointer
Elena Petway, Giant Schnauzer
Godiva Runyon, Labrador Retriever
Roger and Sassy Sikes, Afghan Hounds

GEMINI
May 22–June 21
The Twins
I Think

Right now, Godiva, my Chocolate Lab, is fascinated by a leaf blowing in the wind. It's autumn and she's driving me nuts. I put her outside so she'd relieve herself, but she won't stop staring at the falling leaves. She's more interested in watching them than listening to me.

Come on down, Gemini!

GEMINI, symbolized by THE TWINS, is the third house in the zodiac and the last sun sign in spring. Whereas the earthy Tauruses are fixed in their ways, Geminis anticipate change and while waiting for it they appear nervous or antsy.

Gemini is the first sign with the element of Air. Unlike Tauruses who are down-to-earth and grounded, Geminis are perceived as air heads or space cadets. These descriptions aren't meant to be derogatory. Geminis aren't stupid; they're cerebral, inquisitive, expressive, and inventive. With Geminis, variety is the spice of life. They are nonconforming, versatile, and amusing. Geminis aren't ditzy, they merely march to the tune of a different drummer. These twins should be viewed as being in the twilight zone rather than being candidates for the loony bin!

The Gemini motto is I THINK, but seeing that Geminis, who are symbolized by The Twins, have the element of Air and the need for change, that motto often becomes I THINK/I THINK?

Gemini The TWIN is one of the two dual sun signs. Geminis are said to have more than one personality, which I believe stems from their need for change. Boredom is Geminis greatest enemy. But unlike Aries who will initiate change, Geminis live in anticipation of change. Like the feather in the opening scene of "Forrest Gump," Geminis land, launch, and land again as the breezes blow. What they'll do next will often be a surprise.

Godiva was a rescued dog who unsuccessfully lived in several other homes before I got her. She was wild and unruly and we were just about to look for another placement when Godiva did a complete about-face. Overnight, she became calm and obedient.

Georgia has two speeds, go and go again. If she could, she'd play until dark, then move the activity inside. Even if she's dog tired and can barely walk, much less run, she will continue wanting to frolic. She seems to have no limits as long as she can get an occasional drink of water or a Frosty Paw.

Rush Limbaugh hates inactivity. If he can't find any action, he'll run down to the "pull gate" and attack it because he is bored! When he first learned to work the gate, he was a small puppy. He'd grab the rope and tug and tug until it opened. Rush is as loose as a goose and he never thinks things through. He'll jump on another dog just to stir up some action.

Geminis' element is Air, and when asked if air could be used to describe one's dog, I received these responses:

Talk about air heads! Sassy is beautiful but out of it. You can look in one of her ears and see straight through! I have to place Sassy's food in the same spot every night or she forgets where she's supposed to eat.

Roger is very smart. He's also a big show-off. He became a champion at the age of six months, which is real unusual for an Afghan, but Roger can be a space cadet. He's scared of his own shadow. As a pup, he had a fear of closed doors. If one slid back and forth, raised or lowered, or had to be bar-pushed opened, he'd react as if he'd been shot out of a cannon . . . shell shocked. It was really embarrassing. I'd feel like an idiot carrying Roger into rooms. The worst was lugging him into dog shows. He's better now, thank goodness.

Georgia often gets so caught up in exploring trees, squirrels, etc., that she will walk right into objects in her path. I'm not sure this makes her an air head or not, but she often lies on the floor with her head under the bed and stares at absolutely nothing, sometimes for twenty minutes or more.

Agatha is an air head all right . . . always unsure of her decisions. I'll ask if she needs to go out, open the back door, and she'll go out and immediately turn around to come back in. The older she gets, the worse she is. It drives me nuts.

Elena wants you to think she's an air head so she can simply do as she pleases.

Geminis can be very creative and imaginative. Air signs are motivated by the mind and live in the realm of thought. They have a knack for coming up with quick solutions. A friend of mine told me about her Gemini Dobie. The first time she tied him to a tree, he got his leash all tangled. Dobie looked at his lead, thought a few moments, then literally walked around the tree until he got it untangled. To this day, the dog has been able to solve this kind of problem.

At first, I thought Godiva was dumb as a post, but now I realize she's very smart and just wants to be human.

When Georgia can't get anyone to play with her, she will find two balls, put one in her mouth, and kick the other around the room with her front paws (she actually thinks they're hands) . Quick solutions? She's learned to step on one side of a Frisbee then clench the raised part in her mouth. She's also mastered the ability to flip a June bug with her nose so she can play with it. Unfortunately, she hasn't learned how to revive the insect when she chomps down too hard.

Elena was playing with a ball one day and became thirsty. She ran to the water bowls (I have three other dogs so I keep two bowls filled), which sit on an elevated stand. When she got there, one bowl was empty and the other full. Instead of dropping the ball on the floor, she put it in the empty bowl, took her drink, retrieved the ball, and ran off.

Agatha can figure out how to open any door or cabinet. I've had to put child protectors on everything that opens to keep her out.

One Christmas, Lil Marlene ate a two-pound box of chocolates while no one was home. She threw up but managed to hide each accident. It took me days to realize she'd thrown up seven times. Each one was hidden under places such as the couch, chairs, pillows and rugs.

Geminis are cheerful, playful, and might be described as the perpetual child, and these childlike attributes will accompany them throughout their lives.

Godiva is constantly into mischief. She raids the trash cans, but she's long gone by the time I find my other dog in the mess.

Georgia loves to relieve people of their socks, then does what we call her "sock dance." She will throw a sock up in the air, then spin as she watches it float to the ground. When the sock hits the floor, Georgia bows, picks it up, and tosses it into the air again. Sometimes she'll shake the sock then run from room to room in celebration of her catch. In my mind, Georgia will always look and act like a big puppy. She always seems to smile and loves everyone, even if it means a greeting might leave paw prints on their clothes.

Elena will perform for anyone, and if no one is watching, she will perform for herself. She loves attention. Nothing makes her happier than giving everyone who enters the house a high five.

Agatha is a fourteen-year-old Old English Sheep Dog. She's not only still childlike, she also still pouts when she doesn't get her way.

Geminis are sweet, somewhat indecisive, and inquisitive. They react with wonder. Life is amazing and miraculous. Newness and change are like manna to them.

We don't call her Curious Georgia for nothing. She loves to survey new areas, but even more, she likes watching us do things. The other day, she literally stared at me while I crushed a box to put in the trash. She looked at me as if to say, "I may need to do that one day, so I better pay attention." She's started to take great interest whenever I floss or brush my teeth.

Training your Twin can be a challenge. Geminis love to learn but like doing things on their terms, not yours. Training should take place in an isolated atmosphere. Sessions should be short or varied, or you'll find yourself either whistling or spitting into the wind. Geminis have more fun testing your limits than learning the curriculum. Don't ask them to do something, *tell* them to do it. You can't give these June puppies choices, because none will ever be made. Be stern and firm, and above all be patient. Geminis are smart but remember—you're smarter.

A friend's Gemini failed three obedience classes and two personal trainers. Her dog, she says, may recognize sit, rarely recognizes down, and will fetch if begged.

Godiva has no focus whatsoever. She needs constant reinforcement. Eye contact's very necessary, but it could be worse.

Georgia has no trouble making choices. She will do something for you when she's ready or if it in some way benefits her. She will sit to have her leash put on, she will lie down for a snack, and she will do just about anything for a vegetable or an ice cube. But you can't expect her to do these things without bribing her. She thinks she's the boss, and I almost have to bargain with her to get my way.

I first thought Agatha was insecure, but I soon realized she was easily distracted. It drove me nuts! I had to hold her face between the palms of my hands, stare her straight in the eyes, and tell her what I wanted.

Addie's very moody and will give me "the look" when she's annoyed. Often, I have to convince her to do something. I might as well hang a "I work for food" sign around her neck because that's what it really takes to motivate her. She's difficult because her mind wanders.

Although Elena is not a foodaholic, she will focus quite nicely on puppy bones. However, if a squirrel walks across the yard of a neighbor five houses down the street, she immediately loses attention and starts to hunt, even though she's in the house.

Sassy WILL NOT pay attention! She's untrainable and stubborn.

Roger is a challenge. Roger's moody and whether or not he learns something depends on how he feels that day.

Geminis like conversation and seem to have an almost human grasp of language.

While most dogs seem to hear "blah, blah, blah, good dog," Georgia appears to listen to sentences as if she's diagramming them in her head. If I am channel surfing and Homeward Bound, The Incredible Journey is on, Georgia sits up and becomes impervious to her surroundings like a little kid. And when she watches, it's almost as if she's not only seeing the animals on screen but has to hear their voices so she can understand the plot.

I took Elena to a park with a large lake. Luckily, I had her on a 26 flexi-lead. Although she had never been in water except for a bath, she suddenly sprang into the lake and began swimming. I finally managed to reel her in to shore. She looked at me as if to say: Great granny, why did you fish me out? I was having a ball! Elena has an active vocabulary of about 150 words and she's still very young.

Rush is as smart as his two-legged counterpart. If I rant and rave about whatever, he tends to look and listen as if he's taking it all in. When I stop, he jumps in my lap and gives me lots of kisses. It's as if he's saying "Thank you for giving me such good advice."

With Addie, we have to spell some words so she won't know what we're talking about. She comes about as close to talking to us as you can imagine.

Be warned. There will be times when it will take more than words to make your point.

Lil Marlene had this terrible habit of eating everything in sight. If left alone, she'd jump up on counters and devour anything interesting. This included pencils, ink pens, leather gloves and hats, a belt (she left the silver buckle), even a pound of uncooked bacon. We finally had to set mousetraps on every above-floor surface in the house.

Geminis have a wonderful sense of humor.

Lil Marlene taunts our Maybelline who is a Taurus. Maybelline will inhale her dinner, but Lil refuses to eat hers right away. She'll guard her bowl for up to an hour while watching Maybelline salivate. Lil will also lie on Maybelline's bed instead of her own. Maybelline will pace the floor until Lil decides to move.

During the day, Georgia is constantly getting a choice sleeping spot by simply lying on top of Cody, her housemate, until he moves. At night, Georgia refuses to sleep anywhere but in bed with us. As many times as we throw her off, she waits until we've gone back to sleep and creeps back up. I've caught her a couple of times testing the waters. She first lays her head on the side of the bed to check out the situation, then climbs onto the chest at the foot of the bed, and then creeps slowly, one paw at a time, until she finally lies down between my wife and me. One night, Georgia actually slept on our house sitter's head.

Although I know that Scorpios are considered the most sensual of the sun signs, almost every Gemini owner used the term SEXY when describing their dog. So even though the topic wasn't even alluded to in my questionnaire, I'm going to include these reactions from the participants. I mean, it is their dog's life!

Male dogs think of Lil Marlene as air-rotic. She's very sexy. In fact, Lil has her pin-up poster pose she reserves for her dad. She drapes her crossed front legs over his lap while her hind feet remain on the ground. Then she lays her tilted head upon her paws and looks longingly into his eyes.

Sassy thinks she's either Marilyn Monroe or the poster dog for Victoria's Secrets.

When Georgia looks into a camera, it's almost like she knows she's cuter than everyone else and will be the focus of the shot. We have a glass stereo case and Georgia will stop and stare at her reflection. I think she wants to remind herself how good-looking she is. Georgia will also prance around when she thinks she's being watched.

Last but not least, Gemini's motto I THINK brings to mind the philosopher Descartes' quotation, I THINK THEREFORE I AM. These butterflies need to be free to move and experience the wonderful world that surrounds them. So throw away your net, fasten your seat belts, and enjoy the flight. It might be bumpy, but it will be well worth the trip!

CANCER
The Crab

 GOOD DOGGY:
cautious
devoted
helpful
intuitive
melodramatic
mothering
nurturing
protective
sensitive

BAD DOGGY:
clingy
lazy
manipulative
moody
shy
smothering

PAW PRINTS:
Rocky Baker, Beagle
Lili Birnsteel, German Short-hair Pointer
Caro Eicholtz, Labrador Retriever
Sophie Gordon, Miniature Schnauzer
Emmy Hancock, Labrador Retriever
Katie Horton, Golden Retriever
Zeus Mallory, Boxer
Scout Pregliasco, Vizsla

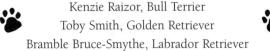

Kenzie Raizor, Bull Terrier
Toby Smith, Golden Retriever
Bramble Bruce-Smythe, Labrador Retriever

CANCER

June 22–July 22
The Crab
I Feel

My dog rides everywhere with me. She sits quietly in the back seat like a perfect lady. I feel as if I'm driving Miss Daisy or, in my case, Miss Lili. We make eye contact through the rearview mirror. Often, she plants her front paws between the two front seats and tries to makeout with me. Lili is as regal as her namesake, Liliuokalani, the last queen of the Hawaiian Islands. Lili is a Cancer, as am I. Between the two of us, there is an emotional attachment that tends toward the absurd.

CANCER the CRAB is the fourth house in the zodiac. It's the first sign with the element of Water and, like water, Cancers will seep into the depths of your being. Cancer is the first month of summer, the beginning of those hazy, lazy, crazy days. Where Aries thrive on a sense of urgency, Cancers thrive on a sense of security. Cancers want to take care of or be taken care of and pampered.

Cancers are emotional, gentle, intuitive, nurturing, and nonviolent. Cancer is the most sensitive of the sun signs. Their motto, I FEEL, often means I

FEEL INSECURE. I FEEL I NEED TO SPEND EVERY WAKING HOUR WITH YOU. I FEEL MY DEVOTION SHOULD BE RECIPROCATED.

Cancer's icon is THE CRAB, and once Cancers get their claws into you they're tough to shake. They expect your attention at all times. This can be annoying, especially when they start following you into places such as the bathroom. It's like, all right already, enough of this togetherness. I cannot leave a room without Lili following me, even when she's spent a lot of time making her bean bag into the perfect nest. If I'm sitting down, she'll get in my lap, even though she weighs 55 pounds, and curl up as if she were a small dog. When I leave her in the car while running an errand, she climbs onto the ledge in the rear window and watches for me. Sometimes, she positions herself on the ledge while I'm driving. People seeing her think it's a riot, but she blocks my visibility and it's hard to see to drive.

Katie's always looking for love and reassurance. When she feels needy, she whines and rolls on her back for a belly rub. Katie needs love every bit as much as she needs food and water. When Katie was younger, she'd check to make sure she knew where I was. The older she got, the more by-my-side she became, and now she's with me at all times.

Toby is under my desk when I'm studying, under the dining room table at dinner, and under our bed at night. He will lie on hot bricks while I'm sun bathing or walk with me through 12-inch snowdrifts in the winter.

I'm a groomer and Zeus will get on the grooming table when I'm working on another dog. He doesn't mind getting wet or having shorn fur flying in his face. He's very insecure. He needs to be with me at all times. As I write this, he's in my lap and it's hard to see over him. Zeus is always brushing up against me, and I constantly have to tell him he's a good boy. If I come into a room, I have to reassure him that whatever he's doing is okay. If I'm on the phone, Zeus will sit in front of me and talk until I hang up. He's done this so much that I've taught him to sing Old MacDonald. *He barks at exactly the right times.*

Sophie is devoted to me and merely tolerates everyone else. She will sit and stare at me until I talk to her. Sophie understands what I'm saying, and always responds appropriately. Sometimes she gets in my face and gives me a kind of silent bark. If that doesn't work, she'll slap me with her paws to get my attention.

No dog could be as devoted as Emmy. Emmy wants to be wherever I am. She stays by my side or with me in sight. Yesterday I took her to my doctor's office. The receptionist could see Emmy pacing in the back seat, watching for me. When I got back to the car, she sat in my lap for about five minutes while I gave her hugs and reassured her that I was okay. When Emmy wants to play and I'm busy, she'll deliberately get something she's not supposed to have, like a shoe, and chew on it in front of me.

Scout will not sleep in a room alone. She will whine if I'm not touching her. She needs a lot of love.

Cancer's element is Water and water signs live in their feelings; their emotions determine their behavior. Seeing that water can take various shapes and can get through, around, under, or into almost anything, you'll find some Cancers are escape artists. Bramble, who lives in the English countryside, will make like Houdini if she's left alone too long.

Bramble is an accomplished escape artist. For many years if we weren't home, she'd actively look for holes in the fencing and, upon finding one, squeeze through. She'd find her way to the closest farm, then have a heady time raiding trash bins and digging around the barns.

Bramble's very best escape occurred while she was left at home when we were on holiday. She got away during exercise period by scaling a security fence. She was found a week later in a village five miles away.

Some Cancers will switch moods rather abruptly. As an owner, you won't even know what sets them off, but these moments rarely last long. Occasionally, you'll find a Cancer as stubborn and obstinate as an iceberg. When Zeus' owner's back gave out while she was in the bathtub, she related this incident.

I called Zeus in hopes of grabbing his collar to pull myself up. Instead, he climbed into the tub and sat on me. I couldn't push him off so there we lay until a friend came over and got us both out of the tub.

Water signs are intuitive and you'll find Cancers are in tune with your emotions as well as their own. But beware. Cancers are quick to exaggerate their own feelings. What starts out as a simple greeting can quickly turn into melodrama.

Bramble was so pleased to be found after her great escape that she put on quite a performance when we got her home. It was almost painful to watch such joy. Ordinarily, Bramble just tears around the garden checking everything and leaping at us in regular intervals. This time, she went through each room in the house to make sure everything was still in place. It was high drama. She also performed every trick she knew, some more than twice.

Zeus jumps and barks. He will bite at my feet and knock things over. Sometimes he will howl as if to tell the world that Mom's come home!

Sophie crows like a rooster. She will interrupt any on-going conversation until satisfied she's been adequately loved. When her groomer came today, I was holding her and she tucked her head against my neck (like a baby would) and would not look at the groomer. She's very entertaining . . . keeps us howling.

Emmy would have been a terrific actress-or is! Everything is melodramatic. She'll act like her life has been totally miserable without me—and the truth is she really believes it.

When I come home, I usually haven't been gone for too long. When my husband comes home from a trip, it's a different story. Caro will look out the back door when she hears his truck pull in and when he opens the door, she is all over him. She does this funny twirl and then she chases her tail.

Scout gets excited even if we've only been gone a few minutes. She'll wag her tail uncontrollably.

Cancers are very gentle. Lili will passively watch deer saunter through our yard, and will ignore a baby bird that's fallen out of its nest. She backed off barking at a baby raccoon that had fallen out of a tree. Of course, its mother hissing at Lili might have something to do with her retreat. When she cornered a ground hog one day, I only had to call her once before she left it.

Whereas some of the sun signs will be quick to tear up their toys, a Cancer won't. Being a nurturer, your Cancer will enjoy stuffed animals. They are soft, cuddly, and satisfy a Cancer's need to protect. Lili still has the same two teddy bears she had as a puppy, and Lili's now four years old. She will worry these toys, but she's never tried to dismember them.

My nephew's toys are never safe when he comes to visit Katie because she gently carries them away and sometimes buries them. Katie has never, ever, destroyed anything. She has this little red devil stuffed animal she's had since she was two, and she's now eleven.

Your toy question is unreal. Zeus is so gentle with his toys. He has a little squeaky ball with a face on it. We call it his Loved One and he actually knows what toy we mean when we speak of his Loved One. When our other dog takes this toy, Zeus will come and tell me. We try not to let the other dog play with the Loved One because Zeus gets very upset when he hears her making it squeak.

Sophie had a toy possum when she was a puppy and never destroyed it. She never chews on the children's stuffed animals, although she sometimes sleeps in my daughter's collection of them.

Emmy has several stuffed animal toys and she loves to play with them. But you're right about being gentle . . . all ears, tails, etc. are still in place—just maybe a little dirty.

Kenzie is the only bull terrier we ever had who doesn't destroy her toys. In fact, she loves to steal our children's toys and make them her own.

Caro is gentle with her stuffed animals at first. Over time, she loves them to death. After she's had them awhile, they start to fall apart. I'm a Cancer too and can't throw anything away, so I still have Caro's unstuffed toys lying around.

Scout loves her stuffed animals and takes them from house to yard and back while fondling them with her mouth and paws.

Cancers hate conflict and, like their icon the Crab, will pull into their shells or side-step confrontations. They will react to arguments as if it were their fault. If Lili thinks she's made us angry, she tries to crawl out of the room. If I yell at her, she seems to turn inside out.

If we argue, Katie paces between us until our differences are resolved. If Katie's scolded, she might try to disappear, but then again, she's very seldom reprimanded for anything.

If I raise my voice to him, Zeus will crawl on the floor to me. He doesn't want me upset. He'll also crawl to me if I raise my voice to anyone else.

Instead of saying Toby's a Golden Retriever, we say he is a Golden Retreater because he's so laid back, sweet-natured, and timid. Conflict would traumatize him. Luckily, our family is pretty peaceful.

Sophie barks and growls when she thinks we are arguing. Generally it's just play, but she perceives it as a threat.

When Caro hears a raised voice, she thinks she is in trouble and will hide under the kitchen table. It's almost impossible to get her to come out.

Food is a great motivator, but unlike Taurus, you won't find many Cancer dogs helping themselves to whatever's on the counter. This is not to say they won't beg for biscuits. Beg, heck, Lili doesn't have to beg. She starts drooling as we turn into the bank parking lot because she knows she'll get a treat or two at the drive-in window. But I can leave her alone in the car with a bag of cold cuts and she won't touch them. Well, maybe she'd think about it, but she wouldn't eat anything.

Cancers are very obedient and protective. They tend to favor either Mom or Dad. In Lili's case, she's devoted to me during the week, but on weekends her heart belongs to Daddy. She won't even look at me, she's so busy following him around.

Cancers are easy to train because they want to make their owners happy. We never took Lili to an obedience class. As a puppy she learned to sit, stay and come immediately. She is also whistle-trained and will turn on a dime to return to me when I blow one. Toby's owner tells me that Toby never goes out of the yard, which is good because it borders a very busy highway. When I took Lili to visit, Toby kept her from getting too close to the road.

Most dogs don't like loud noises, but Cancers seem more sensitive than other sun signs. Noise disrupts the tranquility and serenity of their home sweet home. When the weed eater or lawn mower fires up, Lili comes inside. When the vacuum cleaner's running, out the door she goes.

If Emmy hears something, she runs home. If she hears other dogs barking, she'll come to my feet—usually with her tail tucked. If I get mad at Emmy and shout at her, she'll look at me as if to say, "What's wrong?"

then comes running to my side to comfort me as if the problem were mine and not hers.

Sophie hides in my closet when the cleaning lady comes and when there's a storm. She will not let the dog groomer blow her dry—she screams. A doorbell, even on TV, and slight noises outside bother her.

As sensitive as Cancers are in life, so are they in death. Since this writing, Katie has passed away. Her owner described her as always kind and considerate, the perfect lady, in life and death.

Katie developed a degenerative bone tumor on her leg. I'm sure she knew something was wrong, but we didn't have any indication there was a problem until a week before she died. It was then she started limping. Katie had never expressed any indication of pain, but by then the tumor was so bad her leg had nearly disintegrated. Within a few days, she quit walking. The day before our final visit to the vet, I gave Katie a dog treat which she'd ordinarily take outside to eat. The next afternoon alone, for Katie was gone, I stepped into the back yard Katie had so loved. The biscuit lay on the stoop. It was the only time Katie had not eaten her treat or that it hadn't been buried for later. Next to it lay the little red devil toy she'd had since she was two. I believe this was Katie's way of saying goodbye to me, her way of saying it was okay, it was time for her to go.

Today, Katie's stuffed red devil toy still sits on the stoop where Katie once lay.

LEO

The Lion

 GOOD DOGGY:
ambitious
brave
cheerful
dramatic
enthusiastic
flamboyant
generous
passionate
proud
self-assured

BAD DOGGY:
aloof
bossy
conceited
cowardly
inconsiderate
nosey
pretentious

PAW PRINTS:
Woofie Bell, Yorkshire Terrier
Lizzie Deckard, Golden Retriever
Cuzco Karem, Shepherd/mix
 Gabby Mitchell, Gordon Setter
Boomer Norfleet, Shih Tzu
Oakley Onachilla, German Short-hair Pointer
Woody Sibler, Cocker Spaniel
Spanky Tarrant, Corgi/Beagle

LEO
July 23–August 23
The Lion
I Will

Getting Leo owners to return my questionnaire was like pulling hens teeth. I coaxed and cajoled, but my pleas fell on deaf ears. If and when the questionnaires were returned, they were torn, crinkled, or splashed with coffee or stains of some sort. I began to ponder my predicament and finally realized why I was having so much trouble. Leo is the King of the Canines. People don't own Leos, people serve them, and revealing their dogs' habits and hangups would be the equivalent of treason!

LEO is the fourth house in the zodiac and the second sign with the element of FIRE. Unlike rambunctious Aries who blaze new trails with eyes wide shut, Leos are more cautious and in control. Leo is the middle month of summer, and middle months tend to be set in their ways. Leos like to take time checking out the layout and exploring the unexplored. These kingly cats are most comfortable in their castles. After all, their home is their throne. But Leos are usually game for anything new and are always gung-ho to go. Once someone or some place becomes familiar, Leos consider it their own.

> *When I first took Oakley to the nature preserve, he stayed close to me. With each visit, his range got wider. He now acts as if he owns the place and in a way, he does!*

> *We live in a six-story condominium, and Woofie rules all floors and lords it over the other dogs in our building. Although he's a Yorkie, he acts as*

if he's Richard the Lion Hearted. If he doesn't like something, he will roar his disapproval. If a new dog moves in, Woofie immediately lets him know Woofie's the boss.

Woody likes to sit on the sofa, look out the window, and bark at everything. He also likes to ride in the car, look out the window, and bark at everything. Its like he's saying, that's mine and that's mine and lookie there, that's mine too.

I own an electric fence company. Lizzie's so agreeable that I take her with me on estimates. She now thinks every yard is her yard and she's happy to share each one with the dog or dogs who actually live there.

I teach at a college in Hawaii. My dog Boomer's territory is the campus. Boomer's very courageous and fears no thing and no one. Naturally all the students, his subjects, adore him. If there's a crowd gathered, you can be sure Boomer's in the middle. The kids call him ohdacute as in oh-the-cute-dog.

Leos are very protective of their possessions. Dogs born under this sun sign aren't eager to share their owners with anyone, including another dog. Remember, it's a jungle out there and Leo's the King of the Jungle.

Oakley prances around with his head held high as if he were holding court. Then when the two of us are just sitting, he has his paw on me to show his ownership. So there we sit, like something out of a Dr. Seuss book, The Paw Battle. *He'll put a paw on me and I'll push it away. So he thinks maybe the other paw will have better luck. Pretty soon, he's hunched over on his hind legs with both paws in the air, waiting for that perfect moment to put both of them on me. Then, just when I think he's given up, he'll circle around, lie down, groan, and stick his paw out so it pushes against me as he falls asleep.*

Lizzie is never aggressive. She is a self-confident dog who is very secure in her approach to the world. But if she's bothered by one of my other dogs which she thinks she owns, she silently bares her teeth. There's no growling or follow through . . . just a warning. I haven't a doubt that she would protect any family member if provoked.

Leo's motto is I WILL, and as we all know, where there's a will there's a way! Leo is seen as a domineering sun sign, but appearance is not always reality. Beneath all of that lionhearted bravado, you'll find a real pussy cat.

Lizzie tested as having a low degree of sensitivity on her puppy test. This is true. You can stand on her tail, accidentally of course, and she doesn't get up or respond. But she is as emotionally sensitive as any Golden I've ever owned. A quiet "no" will stop any undisciplined behavior.

Spanky Doodle is very standoffish with strangers. It takes awhile for him to warm up. Although Spanky might seem courageous and act as if he were ten feet tall, if someone were to say "boo" during his posturing, he'd run and hide.

Cuzco is more like a kitten than a cat. It's her brother who's the real Lion. When he comes over, he acts like everything is his, including Cuzco's dog house.

Woody's brave in front of us. A lot of barking and carrying on at home or in the car. But when left alone, he stops barking and becomes meek and mild.

Leos don't like to be left in the dark. Leos are nosey. They always want to know what's going on. Remember that saying about curiosity and cats?

Woody's very nosey. In fact, we tell him we should have named him Snoopy.

Lizzie is very curious and actively uses her nose as if she were a hound.

Oakley will push aside any dog who is digging, then stick his nose into the hole to see what the other dog was after.

Cuzco's very inquisitive. She always sticking her nose into things. She tries to check out all wildlife such as deer, snakes, turkeys, and horses. At night, when we're camping, she listens to all the sounds around her.

Spanky always has to know what's going on . . . what's in here . . . what's in there.

Leos, the most extroverted sun sign, are often referred to as the actors of the zodiac. Whereas Cancers are melodramatic and emotional, Leos are dramatic and intense. Much like John Travolta's character Tony in *Saturday Night Fever*, these August cats like to strut their stuff. They like the nightlife. They love to boogy and they love an audience. They love being center stage. If a Leo doesn't think you're paying enough attention to him, he'll let you know.

Woody wants to be the star. If he thinks I'm ignoring him, he'll use his paws. If I'm standing, he scratches my leg, and if I'm sitting, he'll paw at my arm. He's very insistent.

Lizzie has vocalized since puppyhood. Barking was the initial way she got my attention, later throwing singing in for emphasis. We quickly reinforced only singing, which she now does on cue.

Gabby is very vocal. If she wants to be noticed, she speaks. It's like "Hey, I'm the important one here. Get off that phone!"

Boomer shines! He prances and preens around campus. Boomer loves to entertain and when I sing to him, he dances around like Snoopy. If he gets a burr in his paw, his act becomes one of suffering. He'll limp so pathetically that the students will stand in awe and say, "Ohdacute is so brave!"

Spanky's very dramatic. When someone's eating, he puts on his starving act. He'll sit, ears back, and look completely famished. I must say, it works. He always gets a bite.

Being actors, Leo's love learning new roles. Oakley has a whole slew of tricks he performs. He responds to all the obedience commands, spins around in circles when told to twirl, stops on "whoa," and shakes as if wet when he's completely dry. The first time I saw Oakley do a shake, I was astounded. I asked his owner how she taught him to do that. "Easy," she said. "I just blew in his ear."

Cuzco is very intelligent, but I never taught her any tricks. However, once I tried to get her to carry her own food. On a hiking trip, I gave her a doggie pack. Typically, on the trail she always runs ahead of me. When I put the pack on her, she started lagging behind but stayed close enough to keep hitting my leg. I tried to nudge her up front, to her usual position, but she wouldn't budge. I finally gave up, took off her doggie pack, and she immediately ran ahead. What can I say? The dog's smarter than I am.

Woody has us doing tricks. He won't go down the basement steps, but he loves to run to the door, fling his racquet ball down the stairs, and waits for us to retrieve it. Likewise, he tries to get it stuck under the sofa.

Please, whatever the performance, no negative reactions on your part. Leos need lionizing, not scrutinizing. Making mistakes is Leo's biggest fear and nothing is worse than being booed. Oakley's owner almost changed his name when someone thought she was calling for Ugly. Teasing really hurts a Lion's feelings and only results in tails being tucked. Leos are inordinately fond of praise, and flattery will work wonders. When training, be stern but avoid sarcasm. When your Leo gets it right, yell BRAVO and applaud.

Sometimes on the shake command, Oakley tries to get by with a little shrug like that of the Metro-Golden Meyer Lion. When I repeat the command with emphasis, he gets it right. After I praise him, he prances around looking like the cat who's eaten the canary.

Being extroverted, Leos may seem arrogant and aloof. Often presenting an aura of "Don't mess with me. I'm a fire sign." The don't-play-with-fire attitude surrounds them.

Oakley is definitely not one of those dogs that say hi to everyone. In fact, unless you have wings or feathers or a rare treat (because he is not food driven), he could care less about you and most dogs.

I can pick up Spanky but only when he wants to be picked up. Otherwise he backs off. But if Spanky decides that all is well, he could sit on my lap the rest of his life and allow me to pet him 24 hours a day.

When Gabby feels she's been wronged, she acts very distant. We'll sit in the den at night, and if she feels she hasn't gotten every single thing she believes she deserves, she won't sit where we can see her. Of course, she might be hiding behind the chair so she can sneak into the kitchen in case there's any food left lying around.

When Leos are focused, they're like moths to a flame and either won't listen or will pretend not to hear you. In fact, you might say that Leo's favorite word is ignore. Try not to get mad when this happens, as actors are known to get carried away by their own performance.

Oakley will be loping along, then stop and cock his head as if he hears voices, then . . . he's off! When I say "No, Oakley, no," he acts as if I'm saying, "Go, Oakley, go." I'll call and call. When he finally does return, he'll look at me as if to say, "Okay, I've returned." He'll walk a few steps with me then bam, he's gone again.

When Lizzie's doing something she dearly loves, she acts as if she doesn't hear me when I call. She adores running obstacle courses and the faster she runs, the wilder she gets. It's very funny to watch.

When Leos are on a mission, get out of their way. Oakley's enthusiasm has knocked me off my feet a few times, and he's rolled Lili more than once. You've got to be on your toes as these lions can pounce with no warning.

What Spanky loves to do the most is to lie in wait for Hoover, my unsuspecting Golden, to come running up the hill. Spanky will grab his tail and hold on for the longest time. Hoover, being a Sagittarius, good naturedly goes along with the routine.

So there you go, Leo owners. That's the end of this act. Enjoy your Leos, sing their praise, admire their courage, and groom them until they shine. Leos are always ready for a curtain call, and their dramatic approach to life will bring you hours of viewing pleasure. Remember, these beasty boys are just really cool cats and are a lot of fun to have around! So sit back and bask in their warmth.

Oh, by the way, this note arrived long after I finished this chapter.

"I want to apologize for taking so long to respond to your survey. I also want to say I'm sorry for not being able to return the Leo questionnaire you sent for my sister-in-law. I know you were counting on it, but I gave it to her and she lost it."

Need I say more?

VIRGO
The Virgin

 GOOD DOGGY:
conscientious
diligent
modest
meticulous
perfectionist
precise
shy

BAD DOGGY:
fussy
messy
picky
prissy
temperamental

PAW PRINTS:
Samantha & Moose Cooper, Labrador Retrievers
Stokely Hancock, Labrador Retriever
 St. James Matzek, Benji/Mutt
Hope Rademaker, Sheltie/Mix
Polly Stewart, Jack Russell Terrier

VIRGO
August 24–September 22
The Virgin
I Analyze

I had a lot of trouble writing this chapter until I realized that Virgo is the only sun sign with a human icon. After that, it was easy. I simply translated dog-speak to people-speak so you could read their own words.

VIRGO is the Sixth House in the zodiac and the only sign with a human icon, THE VIRGIN. VIRGO'S motto is I ANALYZE, which reveals their most irritating trait: they are picky, picky, picky. VIRGOS' fussiness gives them the reputation of being high-strung. Being persnickity, coupled with their element EARTH, makes the definition of Virgo a contradiction of terms. How can Virgos be high-strung yet down-to-earth? It's easy. Picture Felix Unger of the *Odd Couple.* He's compulsive in his quest for cleanliness and order, but he's also the shy homebody who takes the back seat when his roommate Oscar Madison's around. Oscar's the slob, a Felix gone bad, while Felix is the perfectionist. Felix might debate making his bed if he gets up to pee in the middle of the night while Oscar has never made a bed in his life. Take both to a hamburger joint and Felix will order steak tartare. Large crowds make Felix uncomfortable. If the magazines on the coffee table are askew, he'll straighten them. Now, change Felix into Fido and you'll have . . . a Virgo.

HOPE
Hello. My name is Hope. I am Sheltie and people say I look like a little Lassie, but I'm gray and white while she was brown and black. Anyway, I'm a little nervous writing this for you. I am shy when it comes to new

acquaintances or experiences and, believe me, this is a new experience. I'm more the old shoe member of my family. I'd rather hang back or get behind Mommy than write about myself, but she said it will help build my self-confidence. Oh here I am rambling again. Mommy says I need to cut to the chase.

Mommy's other dog was brutally run over twice by drunken drivers. She said that all she had left was Hope, which she named me. Mommy says I was a tiny little puppy with a gigantic heart. She says I'm the sweetest, most loyal, lovable, good, kind, and beautiful family member. She tells people that I came with wonderful manners of minding, and never running off even if the gate were left open. Mommy thinks I'm perfect. To thank her, I give her hugs by pressing my muzzle against her cheek.

I want everything to go according to schedule. I like a routine. Knowing the plan is important to me because I need to complete a task correctly. I always look before I leap. I never had to be housebroken. Mommy took me outside when I was five weeks old, told me what to do and why, and that was that.

I am very fussy and will examine anything that's given to me. I don't want anything out of place. I want to eat from my food dish only. I want dinner served at the same time and in the same spot every day. My comfort towel and seal stuffed toy have to be arranged in just the right manner and kept in the same place. I have to know where my seal is when it's time for bed, because I have to go and shake him before I go to sleep. My bedtime is always 9 o'clock.

Noise bothers me. I don't like it when the phone rings. I leave the room when Daddy starts clicking the remote. Cymbals in any musical recordings drive me to distraction, and I don't like tools that make bang-

ing noises. I prefer soft voices, and when someone is talking too loud, I have to bark and bark until they tone it down. I want peace and tranquility. When the vacuum cleaner's running and the phone rings or the washing machine's off balance and Mommy doesn't hear, I'll alert her by barking so she'll shut them up.

Stress makes me ill. I thought I'd die when Mommy packed up all those boxes when we moved. I couldn't help it—I started chewing my paw. Mommy tried to bandage it, but it didn't do any good. I chewed right through the tape.

It troubles me when Mommy's car is in the shop and Daddy parks in her space. The absolute worst was when Granddaddy died. I couldn't believe he was gone. For months, I'd run into his house and up the stairs looking for him. Also, I hate it when I'm left alone. I pout if we go for a drive and Daddy comes along because I have to sit in the back seat.

Mommy says I've saintly manners. I always walk with my head held high and people constantly stop to tell me how pretty I am. If by chance they forget, I stretch my front paws and bow to remind them to fuss over me.

Mommy says I talk by the looks I give and I communicate through body language. I understand everything Mommy says when she's with someone or on the phone. When we're on walks, Mommy always talks to me, and when she says something like "there's an airplane," I know to look up. When she tells me someone's going to stay with me while she's away, I get sad and pace in anxiety about her departure.

Mommy takes me to a place called Henry's Ark. Henry rescues zoo and other kinds of animals. They live on his farm and anyone can visit and play with them because they are, as Mommy says, user-friendly. I go there and I rub noses with the zebras, water buffalo, cows, donkeys, and ponies. If there are babies there, I'm very careful and gentle with them. The only thing I don't like there is the ostrich. He's kind of a stinker!

Connecting with my family is of utmost importance, and I don't like things that separate us, things which mean they're leaving me, like bicycle wheels, skateboards, and roller blades. I hate waiting for Mommy when she stops to talk for a long time when we're on walks, because I get bored.

I adore the smell of fresh flowers, the taste of fresh cool water, and being able to relax in my own home. I love being brushed, washed, and having my coat blown dry. Mommy gives me massages and rubs sweet smelling lotions on me. When my mouth is dry, she puts lip balm on my lips. I let Mommy cut tangles out of my ears and administer any kind of medical attention. If I'm hurt and have to go to my dog doctor, I'll sit at Mommy's feet in the reception room while she holds my front paw. If Mommy's ill, I'll stay by her bed and will not leave. I have to be there to check out every bit of food, drink, or medicine that is brought to her. I let her know I'm by her side by having some part of me touching her. Mommy says I'm her sweetheart, her best pal, and her soul mate.

JAMES

Hello, my name is St. James. I know, it's a pretty aristocratic name for a mutt Terrier who looks like Benji. Well, I was named after this art fair where Mother got me. Go figure. I've no earthly idea why she came home with me instead of art.

I admit I'm another high-strung Virgo. I can't seem to get my body to stop its constant wagging. Mother is always saying, "Calm down, James, you're too energized. You're wound up like a top.

Basically, I'm a great dog. I'm considerate and will always grab a toy to share from my toy basket if someone comes to the door. I like my toys kept in the basket because I can't tolerate disorder. I can't stand it when the house is a wreck unless of course, I've made the mess. For example, I get nervous when I'm left alone. I tear things up. I particularly love trashing the trash cans and shredding toilet paper. I know how to grab a sheet or two and pull the roll all around the condo. It's a lot of fun until Mother comes home and I get this "Oh James, not again" attitude.

I run this household. My people know not to expect too much out of me, so they don't demand too much. If Mother's not ready for bed at my usual bedtime, I'll hop in and go to sleep without her. However, Mother still doesn't understand how much I hate going out in the rain. When she thinks I have to urinate, she'll carry me outside and deposit me on the wet grass. Even the horrified look I give as my body recoils into the fetal position fails to foil her. The tone in her voice used to tip me off and I'd run and hide before she could get me. Now she gives me no warnings. She just silently swoops down and picks me up and out we go. When the weather's good . . . well that's another story. I love to go on walks. Actually, I get obnoxious and excited if she says the word walk. If I'm ready to go out and Mother is not, I'll lie down and sigh dramatically. I like getting what I want. If Mother's climbing the stairs too slowly, I'll grab the handle on the retractable leash and take myself to the top.

Mother knows but occasionally she forgets to tell the bank tellers not to bother giving me their treats. I refuse to touch those awful dog biscuits they hand out at the drive-through window. As far as I'm concerned, they're not fit for animal consumption. Actually, most pet foods aren't fit for animal consumption. No sir, give me people food such as carrots, meat, potatoes, or cookies . . . anything but dog food.

Mother says I'll eat anything. She says I have a stomach of iron. Heck, when I ate that half bag of Halloween Snickers, she didn't even call the vet because she knew it wouldn't faze me. And it didn't. Isn't Mother wise?

I'm not a tough guy, and I like to assess a situation before I participate. There are a couple of dogs downstairs I'd rather not associate with, so I pull back from them and gyrate like that wild and crazy Steve Martin. I know they think something's wrong with me. I'll lunge in their direction and bark my tough dog bark . . . but only after they're out of sight. It took me awhile when we first moved to realize that all the noises coming from the outside hall were not my problem. They were the other residents coming and going. But what did they expect me to do? I didn't know they weren't outside ready to invade my new home. I had to bark.

If there's an argument, I'll cower and slink out of the room. Mother says it's because I assume I've done something wrong. But I'm not a dumb dog. I know when I'm in the dog house. After all this time living here, if someone comes over, I'll tear around, circling all the rooms in the condo. It makes me seem precious, which is what I am.

POLLY

I'm Polly, a Jack Russell Terrier. You know, like Eddie on Frazier except I'm a girl, ha ha. Actually, I am a little nervous sharing myself with you. Jack Russells are known as highly energized dogs. Well, I'm energized around my home, but when I'm not there I'm very, very shy. The people at my kennel call me Shy Polly.

I am a good girl and do whatever Mama and Poppa want me to do . . . NOT. Okay, sometimes if I've got some critter up a tree, it might take a few minutes to obey a Polly-come-here, but for the most part, I do what I'm told.

Once she realized I was never going to jump into a car, Mama started calling me her Little Princess. Jumping into a car is so, so, undignified. Why, I blush just thinking about it. When Mama carries me, I look up at her like Scarlett looked at Rhett Butler as he carried her up those stairs.

I'm fussy about what I eat. Mama knows I will turn up my nose at anything made just for dogs, but she also knows I'll eat a Goldfish cracker in an instant.

I really can't be bothered with strangers, but I love being the center of attention when company comes over. When we have guests, I can't help but squeal with delight. I get up on the couch and wiggle until I'm petted. Mama tells her friends that I'm obnoxious. Pooh on Mama.

When Mama had the audacity to remodel our home, I almost had a fit! I spent the entire time under her bed. It was so awful, all that noise and dust and those filthy carpenters smoking cigarettes and using nasty words. They didn't do that when Mama was around, but I heard what they said when she left. I was afraid if I weren't hiding, they might actually try to pet me. The thought of their pawing, I mean handling, my poor body makes me cringe.

Mama says I'm pathetic when I'm stressed, and she's right. I hate it when things are out of order. If one of our garbage cans rolls into our neighbor's yard, I go crazy. I can't stand autumn when all those leaves fall off the trees, all that clutter of leaves on the ground. If something blocks my view when I'm looking out the window, I growl. I also can't be

in the same room with Mama when she's folding the laundry or making
a bed. I'll only go in when everything is tidy again.

Mama says I'm agile, that I leap like a gazelle when I'm hunting. I
think that's a good image, but I'm not sure. I have a hard time with lan-
guage. Unlike most Virgos, I don't know a lot of words. I do know stay,
walk, cookie, no, Gigi (that's my grandmother), and garbage. I trust you
won't share this information about my not understanding a whole bunch
of words with anybody else.

I love looking pretty and having my own groomer/beautician, Kitty
our Cat. She washes my neck, ears, and will give me a facial upon
demand.

Rarely will you hear an unkind word said about a Virgo. They are reliable
and dependable, although they do tend to be picky. Moose and Samantha,
Chocolate Lab littermates, prefer their dog food seasoned with chicken broth
and served at just the right temperature.

Virgos are quiet pets and don't like being the center of attention. Conflict
makes them uneasy.

While all my other dogs are jumping up and down, Stokely sits quietly
and thumps his huge tail. He knows he'll get my attention in due time. I
live alone so Stokely's not around scenes or arguments. But if I'm mad at
one of my other dogs, Stokely wants no part of it. He'll leave the room
so as not to be involved.

Like Taurus and Capricorn, Virgo needs a routine. Moose and Samantha
wake up at 6:30 every morning no matter what.

Virgos are cautious, so don't put them on shaky ground. They want their element, Earth, under their feet at all times. Most Virgos have a distinguished gait but like those born under the sign of Taurus, you can't rush them along. As Stokely's owner writes, "He's a slowpoke. He kind of lollygags along."

So there you go, Virgo. These lovable canines will bring much joy into your life. They are conscientious, modest, meticulous, and patient. . . our little virgins.

LIBRA
The Scales

GOOD DOGGY:
balanced
charming
compassionate
cooperative
diplomatic
peacemaker
refined
sociable

BAD DOGGY:
apathetic
devious
indecisive
selfish
shallow
unbalanced

PAW PRINTS:

Angus Crisler, Scotch Terrier
Perro Doe Dog, West Highland White Terrier
Rascal Johnson, Poodle/Mix
 Bruiser Koran, Boxer
Amanda Lomicka, Bouvier Des Flanders
Venetzia Meador, Standard Poodle
Willy Parrish, Terrier/Mix
Trini Petway, Standard Schnauzer
Hauser Skelton, Golden Retriever

LIBRA

September 23–October 23
The Scales
I Balance

One night while having dinner at a local restaurant, I overheard a woman talking about her dog. Apparently, whenever she was getting ready to go out, her dog followed her around, visibly upset that she was about to leave. I couldn't help but ask if her dog were born in October. She thought a moment, then said yes. Your dog's a Libra, I told her. Of all the sun signs, Libra most hates to be left alone.

LIBRA, the southern constellation between Virgo and Scorpio, is the seventh house in the zodiac, the first month of fall and the second sign with the element of AIR. Libra's motto is I BALANCE, and its icon is THE SCALES, the only inanimate icon within the 12 houses. Putting these attributes together, one might picture Libra as an aloof, cool canine, a most righteous soul. Well, jump not to that conclusion because Libra is influenced by the planet Venus. Just as the element of Air breaths life, VENUS brings love to the Libra personality. Could be confusing, so read on.

To understand LIBRA, one thing must be kept in mind: the word libration, which means to oscillate or to move back and forth. If Libra's scales are balanced, Libra will be a loving and cooperative canine who is refined, diplomatic, gracious, and sociable. Libras want nothing more than to please.

Perro, my West Highland Terrier, was a charmer. He ingratiated himself with staunch dog haters. Grown men, who said they'd never be seen with a small rat like Perro, wound up falling totally in love. Perro was very adaptable. If I told him what to do, he would oblige. In fact, this dog would have walked on his hind legs and talked if I asked it of him.

Perro would have loved to be joined to me at the hip. I used to forget he was with me. He'd just be happy sitting under a chair or next to me in the car. His biggest fear was being left alone. Everything else paled by comparison.

Unbalanced or oscillating Libras will be indecisive, easily distracted, self-centered, and stubborn. Instead of wanting to please you, they want you to please them. These Libras like having their own way, and if their scales are askew, it had better be in their direction.

What Amanda dislikes is not having her own way. If another dog refuses to play by Amanda's rules, she'll simply ignore him and resume her activity solo. Her feelings are: My way or the highway.

When Angus doesn't want to go for a walk, it's like dragging a bag of rocks. Sometimes he goes out of his way to be obstinate.

Trini wants nothing but to be pleased. She's quite demanding and very vocal.

Willy has a mind of his own. Sometimes he comes when he's called, sometimes he doesn't. The more you want him to do something, the more determined he is not to do it.

It's important to remember the influence of the planet Venus. In Roman mythology, Venus was the Goddess of Love and Loveliness. You'll find most dogs born under the sign of Libra are very beautiful. But again, beware. Libra is said to be the most self-centered of the sun signs. A Love Goddess expects to be worshiped and Libra is no exception. Libra is content when Libra is the center of attention. When Libra is happy, everyone is happy. When Libra is unhappy, you will find yourself bending over backward to accommodate them. How many times have you asked yourself, "Why am I doing this? Geeze, Fido's just a dog!"

Amanda has this thing about stairs. She wouldn't even use them until she was over six months old. When she began sleeping in our room, I had to carry her upstairs, much to my husband's amusement. When she got to be over sixty pounds, I could no longer lift her. After a war of wills, I finally taught Amanda how to climb the stairs, but to this day she will occasionally sit and whimper until someone gets her.

Willy, my Terrier mix, hates to go out in the rain. I've tried holding an umbrella and carrying him outside, but when I put him down he makes an immediate u-ey to get back to the house. I'll drag him out again, but he'll run and pull to get inside. I did fool him once by fastening a grocery bag over him. I poked a big hole for his head and put his front paws through the hand loops. He liked it once, but the second time I tried, he balked.

Once I left Trini in the car while I went into K-Mart to exchange a video. While I was standing at the customer service counter, a woman ran up yelling, "There's a blue station wagon in the parking lot and a dog's driving it!" Rushing outside, I saw Trini sitting erect in the driver's seat, backing out of the parking place. Luckily, I was able to unlock the car in time to keep it from hitting a Porsche. I guess she got tired of waiting for me.

Libra is the sun sign most concerned with partnerships. It's as if they're incomplete without another in their life. This time, keep THE SCALES in mind. It takes two to balance. If you leave Libras by themselves, expect the consequences, because Libras hate to be left alone.

Amanda, wants to be close by which ever person is home and will usually follow that person from room to room to monitor his/her behavior.

Angus hated being left alone. I'd pen him in the kitchen and he'd chew up everything except the kitchen sink—floor tiles, wall boards, mop and broom handles, you name it. One day, I came downstairs and noticed a strong smell. Angus had gotten into my spices, stored on a microwave cart, and chewed through a plastic bottle of garlic salt. Even after giving him a bath, for days we knew when Angus was around. He stopped with the spices after getting into a bottle of black peppercorns, but he still hates being alone.

Bruiser does not like to be separated from family members. If I close a door, he'll stay there until I come out.

Rascal hates being alone. Once he unwrapped all our Christmas gifts, and another time he pulled strips of wallpaper off the wall.

When anyone leaves the house, Willy causes a large disturbance by growling and barking. When everyone is gone, he shreds toilet paper, turns over trash cans, drags laundry out of the laundry baskets, and generally makes a mess.

After I got my standard poodle Venetzia, she would sit and stare into space as if longing for someone to share her life. I soon got another dog to keep her company.

Venetzia's owner did the right thing. If you have to leave your Libra by himself for long periods of time and you have the room, I'd think about getting another dog. I didn't say do it, I said think about it. Also, you might consider a house sitter instead of a kennel when you go out of town.

Another similarity with their symbolic Scale of Justice, Libras need order in their court. They are happy with harmony, which often comes in the form of a routine. As with Taurus, change can be disturbing.

Bruiser, my Boxer, has set patterns. He has to go out after eating, even if he just came in to eat. When he wants in, he taps on the door. He's very impatient. He wants it now.

Angus wants routine with no disruptions. Otherwise he gets upset. He doesn't like it when I move furniture, do spring cleaning or change his routine.

Willy notices when something's out of place or new. He will growl at it and cautiously approach or stare at it until I show him it's all right. Last fall, we gathered apples, bagged them in plastic bags, and left them out overnight. The next morning , Willy growled and razor-backed at the bags. I showed him what they were, but he still growled and continued to do so even when he was inside the house. We think he's very smart to notice things . . . but weird, too.

Most Libras love to be groomed and pampered. As Willy's owner writes:

> *Willy loves the attention of grooming and will usually roll over for me to wash him with a warm wash cloth. Sometimes he will show his teeth when I clean his feet, but I've determined those are his ticklish spots. He doesn't like it, but he tolerates it. You can make him mad, though, if you keep doing it.*

Then there are Libras who would rather splash through a mud puddle than go around one. These dogs don't think cleanliness is next to Godliness. Amanda's owner writes:

> *Puddles were made for splashing through and if one is really hot, for lying down and wallowing in. Amanda is at her absolute best when in her Pig Pen state—muddy, full of burrs, with outhouse breath.*

In the same paragraph, Amanda's owner gives a good example of the Libra need for balance.

> *Amanda will NOT get into a swimming pool. She has been in the pool twice, and entered on her own accord by using the steps. Cheerfully, she dog paddled like hell all the way around, then tried to exit at the side, standing on her tiptoes and searching furiously for the steps! Both times, she had to be rescued by a fully clothed human. Further attempts to teach her the location of the steps were met with gargantuan resistance and 85 pounds of dead weight.*

Amanda's problem is due to not having stairs located at both ends, giving her that much-needed sense of balance. This is the same problem she has with household stairs. If there is a banister on both sides, she's fine. If there is only one railing, she balks.

Being social, Libra loves nothing more than having a good time. You might say they're real party animals.

Amanda attended her first party when she was a year old. In no time at all, she was greeting every guest, barking and growling her happy growl. She gets ecstatic, dances around, and wags her tail (which she has very little of) while spreading slobbery kisses to all within reach.

Angus is so happy to see anyone. He adores people—young, old, it makes no difference to him.

Willy thinks that anyone who comes over comes over to see him.

Bruiser's a social butterfly, particularly with family members. He gets very excited and tears around the house in circles.

As mentioned, Air signs have the ability to communicate and have a great grasp of words. Whereas the Air in Gemini tends toward the cerebral, Libras let their wants and needs known by being vocal.

Amanda was the Puppy from Hell. We got her in Chicago and she howled like a banshee during the six-hour drive home. This somewhat intense form of communication went on for weeks. She howled morning, noon, and night and then in the middle of the night. She was dogged in

her demands for attention which, I admit, I gave her. She became slav-
ishly attached to my side, telling me her troubles about the crate, the
food, the poor living conditions, and her total lack of freedom. Nothing
stopped her overwhelming need to bitch at me. We began to call her
Demanda.

Unlike picky Virgos, Libras are starved not only for affection but, in many
cases, for food.

Amanda likes to check out the delicacies being served in other dogs'
homes and will lick their bowl clean in a heartbeat. During parties, she
zones in on those likely to be sloppy eaters then stands near them and
waits for morsels to drop.

Rascal's owner says Rascal would wear a birthday hat just to get cake frosting
and that he loves apples, green beans, oranges, etc. Trini's referred to as a
canine Hoover/Eureka whose epitaph will read *Never Missed a Meal.* Bruiser's
owner writes that he eats quickly then licks his dish until all traces of his
meal have disappeared.

A mixed terrier should top out at about 16 pounds. Willy weighs 35
pounds and has rolls of fat. His owner writes that not too many dogs have
love handles on their back sides.

Does your dog seem cool and aloof one moment, then warm and sensitive
the next? Libras can blow as hot or cold as their element of air, making you
feel as if you're dealing with two dogs instead of one. I know I'm being redundant, but it's back to balancing. Whereas the dichotomy of Geminis applies
more to a change in personality, Libra's applies to a change in moods.

In her early puppy days, Amanda complained to anyone who came over. It was embarrassing and soon nobody stayed long if they bothered to come at all. She was hyperactive, irritating, and starved for attention. Amanda finally stopped complaining when we discovered the value of long, strenuous cardiovascular activity. It was like she put herself on quaaludes. By the time she celebrated her first birthday, she was a changed dog. People who saw her as a puppy would ask if it were the same dog because she was so mellow!

Angus's moods vary a great deal. He can go from being very loving and wanting attention to being aggressive to the point of being wild, and then turn around and calmly ignore us all.

Hauser, our female Golden Retriever, was 2½ when our male dog came to live with us. He was her size but she deferred to him and from that point on, let him follow us everywhere rather than doing it herself.

In sum, Libra symbolizes beauty, love, partnership, and peace. They are creative and have a sense of humor, often making you laugh.
Perro's owner writes about his getting into some pots of paint one day and looking extremely pleased with himself with green, yellow, and ocre patterns all over his white coat.

Yes, sometimes Libra's scales may go awry, but you can help restore their balance once you realize what's out of whack. Just remember, being unbalanced frustrates them as much as it does you. Oh, and please . . . don't leave them alone.

SCORPIO

The Scorpion

 GOOD DOGGY:

aware
determined
intense
investigative
mysterious
motivated
passionate

BAD DOGGY:

calculating
jealous
possessive
sneaky
spiteful
suspicious
temperamental

PAW PRINTS:

Bayley Florence, German Shepherd
Winston Farmer, Yorkshire Terrier
Thor Haraf, Dalmatian
Mandy Johnson, Shih Tzu
Dusty Kinsman, Golden Retriever
Uther McDermott, Rottweiller
Libby McGavic, Golden Retriever
Dixie Oliver, Jack Russell Terrier
Cannon O'Neil, Poodle/Beagle/Mix
Winston Russell, Boxer
Tiara Swope, Border Collie

SCORPIO
October 24–November 22
The Scorpion
I Desire

When my friend wrote me a heart-wrenching letter about the death of her Rotteweiler, Uther Pendragon, I was in tears. I was surprised by my reaction. Since he had been a pup, Uther always made me feel on edge. I never trusted him, even when I walked him when his owner was out of town. It wasn't his breed that made me uncomfortable. Her other Rottie was a real sweetheart whom I adored. When she told me Uther's birth date, it all made sense. Uther Pendragon was a Scorpio.

SCORPIO, the eighth house in the zodiac, is passionate, strong-willed, intuitive, mysterious, secretive, and sly. It is the most hard-to-get-to-know of the sun signs because it operates on "gut knowledge," which follows its own inscrutable logic rather than reason. Scorpio is symbolized by the SCORPI-ON, a nocturnal arachnid that has the ability to sting. Scorpio's motto is I DESIRE and usually whatever Scorpio wants, Scorpio gets . . . the ultimate persistent pooch.

Scorpios are known as the detectives of the zodiac, and have the reputation of being sneaks. Being sneaky is Scorpio's way of making sure he gets what he wants. Don't think of this as being selfish. Scorpios aren't malicious, they're clever! Getting what they want is challenging. If Scorpios are successful, they win their case. Victory adds to their self-esteem, and enforces their reputations as sleuths.

Mandy steals anything and prances off with her tail in the air.

After a deer hunt, while processing the venison, I caught a black and white blur out of the corner of my eye. Tiara had snatched a nice chunk of tenderloin.

Cannon likes to sneak into people's bedrooms and make off with socks or a child's stuffed toy. He'll also steal food off unattended tables.

The moment my back is turned, Libby will open the pantry door and head for the dog food canister. If undetected, she'll eat until she makes herself sick.

If you tell Winnie no when he is doing something bad, he watches you, and when you're not looking, he'll keep doing it. He also takes things and hides them like my fingernail polish or his water dish.

Dusty does a lot of sneaky things. As soon as we leave, he's on the sofa or in an armchair. When he hears the car returning, he jumps down to the floor with an innocent look or yawn, like, "I've been dozing here all night!" I can't leave food on the counter if I'm not at home. Dusty's been known to eat a dozen homemade rolls left wrapped in foil. He also ate most of a loaf of bread. Once he retrieved a fish head, hid it in his mouth, and snuck it into the house.

Bayley will wait until we're preoccupied, then steal the food off our plates with absolutely no signs of remorse while being scolded.

Scorpio is a Water sign and the element of water is important in understanding a Scorpio. Water signs live within their feelings. Emotions determine their behavior. However, unlike melodramatic Cancer and reflective Pisces, Scorpios' intensity puts them in a continual power play. In fact, it seems as if they can read your mind, but hey, water represents intuition. As one owner writes:

"Last summer my sister from California stayed with me for a week. She is somewhat into the new age thing and really believes in . . . shall we call it ESP or the paranormal? One day after a slight altercation with Winston, my sister looked at me and said, "That dog knows exactly what I'm thinking!"

So what do we have here? The dog from Hell? Not at all. I call Scorpios our little devils or our love bugs. Just remember that sometimes these love bugs can bite. Let's put it this way: When Scorpios are good, they are very, very good, but when they are bad, they are better.

As the saying goes, still waters run deep. When your Scorpio seems hard to fathom, go below the surface. His belligerence shouldn't be taken personally, it's just that he's in one of his moods. Give him a smile and a pat and tell him to lighten up. If that doesn't work, leave him alone. He'll come out of it, and in no time will be back to being his impetuous and playful self.

Scorpios like to be under pressure and thrive on variety. Give them challenging tasks. Don't be predictable. Scorpios love the element of surprise. Their intensity makes them fiercely loyal and loving companions. Being idle is not Scorpios' idea of the fun. When bored, they can be sly, devious, and manipulative, which puts them in a constant state of alert. Don't let this discombobulate you and don't interpret this as threatening. Most of the time, Scorpio enjoys getting a rise out of you. It puts him in the alpha position.

Scorpios are ego-oriented, but in a way that's dissimilar from Aries. The Aries' "self" results in a childlike approach and an eagerness to experience the world around them. Scorpio's ego involves their desire to control. Their me becomes mine, and it can result in their being obsessive and possessive and downright stuck-up.

Bayley intimidates smaller animals and struts her stuff when she knows people are talking about her. She is very proud, and if she's done something wrong, she celebrates her errors by taking a magician's bow.

I should have named Mandy Ms. Haughty!

Winston is a fawn and white Boxer with a mug the color of a five-o'clock shadow. Winston's dad describes him as "a handsome dude who seems to know it." Winston likes to challenge authority, and his interaction with other dogs always involves control.

Winston will "buzz" whomever I'm walking with. He'll run off for awhile, then come charging toward my companion at full speed. It's as if he's telling them to stay away from me. If Winston sees a dog loose, he grabs its leash and leads the dog around. He also likes to chase dog tails. I think it amuses him to know that they can't bite his back.

Winnie, my Yorkie, attacks bigger dogs without thinking twice! He prances around and always seems so proud of himself.

Dixie is downright bossy with me and other dogs in general.

Again, I remind you that owning a Scorpio isn't always easy. How you react can be the deciding factor in your dogs' behavior. For example:

When Winston snapped at me during our first obedience class, I never returned.

Thor obeys on his own sweet time. I took him to obedience school and the instructor said she never had a Dalmatian graduate. Thor heard her and became the star pupil!

If Winston's owner had returned to class, who knows what the outcome would have been. Winston might, too, have been a star pupil. Then again, he might have been given a dunce cap. With Scorpio, one can never be sure of the road to take, but hey, that's life. Nobody said it was going to be easy.

Let's return to the symbol of this sun sign for a moment. As said, the scorpion is an arachnid, which also applies to spiders. Spiders spin webs to attract what they want while a scorpion's tail is capable of stinging or inciting something to action. All this, plus the fact that scorpions function best in the dark, gives this sign power to put a lot over on mere mortals. Again, Scorpio needs to control.

Uther didn't like anyone getting too close to me and would occasionally challenge me for the alpha position. There were three significant episodes, all occurring after large groups had gathered in my home. After these meetings, irritated, Uther would inevitably challenge my position and try to usurp my control. He wouldn't obey. He never got vicious though, and once confident that I had the upper hand, he'd back down. As a nine-year-old boy summed it up, "Uther takes his job too seriously." I must say, Uther handled defeat with dignity.

No one outside the family has ever touched Thor without my being present. Then he's a doll. If we have company, Thor literally sits on their feet so if they move, he knows it. But if I'm not home, UPS, FedEx and USP packages are left at my neighbor's, or I'm left with a note which reads something like, "Undeliverable, vicious dog." The chimney sweep had to yell for help because Thor wouldn't let him get off the roof.

Libby wants her share of attention and will nudge our other dogs away.
Then she oozes her way into my lap—all 70 pounds of her. Although
she's forced to share me, she clearly prefers not to. At night, she's the clos-
est cuddler on the bed.

Although your Scorpios will seem to know your every thought, reading
their minds might be difficult. Water has the ability to penetrate, find its way
over, under, around, or through obstacles. Water signs are not easily deflected
or diverted. There is nothing shallow about Scorpios and they change course
in a heartbeat. For example, "Dixie can go from being cool and calm, to rav-
ing maniac in a nanosecond," as can Dusty when he sees squirrels, other dogs
or cats. When this happens with Bailey, it's like she has two personalities.
Libby's owner tells me that occasionally Libby will light into one of her other
dogs for no good reason. Well, you might not know the reason, but you can
bet there is one. Remember, you have to look below the surface.

Uther had a personality change after having knee surgery when he was
three years old. After the surgery and subsequent six-month recovery
period, this personality turnabout occurred with regularity. I never knew
how he'd react to other people or dogs . . . devil or angel.

While the staff at Thor's doctor's office were fussing over him and feed-
ing him snacks, Thor spied a Shepherd getting too close to me. Suddenly,
he snarled and grabbed the Shepherd by the neck. As soon as we pulled
him off, he quieted down.

Training your Scorpio will require channeling their energy into acceptable
behavior. As with all dogs, remember you're the boss. Scorpios don't like to be
yelled at, but a firm tone of voice will work wonders. Make eye contact and let

them know you understand where they're coming from. Also remember, Scorpios love to be challenged. Turn that sit-stay routine into an obstacle course. Surprise them with unexpected commands. Hide that ball you want them to fetch. Let them be the sleuths; it's their nature. Stare soulfully at them. Or if your Scorpio's being difficult, give him your best evil eye. Glare! Your tone of voice has to be firm and commanding. End any negative flow by being a block of ice. Unlike with Cancers who are best controlled by a warm flow of words, give your Scorpio looks that can freeze! Be firm while letting them know they are loved, and they will unconditionally love you back. Exercise will help alleviate some of Scorpio's intensity. Remember that under all that posturing and aura of aloofness, Scorpios are, as I've said, our love bugs.

> *As to being sensitive, yes, Dusty is extremely sensitive. Thunderstorms and lightning drive him wild. Several times he's gone into the bathroom during a storm and managed to get the door closed but then couldn't get out! He'll pace and pant during storms. He also has separation anxiety. When the suitcases come out and the packing begins, he gets very nervous and will walk around with a squeaky toy in his mouth or lie down and look pitiful!*

> *Thor is protective of our cats and horses. He demands equal attention when the cats are around, but he's gentle, protective, and will let me know if anyone's in trouble. Thor's also very jealous of our horses. For all Thor's toughness, he's still a sensitive guy. He loves to swim with the Canada geese which land in our pond. The geese don't mind it a bit.*

With Scorpio, sensitivity turns into sensual and intensity turns into passion. Scorpio has the reputation for being the most sexual of the sun signs. When I asked about Winston the Boxer's desires, his dad replied, "Winston's very sexual."

"So, like what, he humps your leg?" I asked.

"Oh no," he said, rolling his eyes. "He goes for little kids, like four-and-five-year-olds. Their parents are aghast."

"Well, I imagine," I replied.

"But the funny thing is, the kids think Winston's dancing with them. I call it his inappropriate dance."

Libby, once in season, was totally obnoxious to my daughter's neutered male. He looked as if to ask, "What am I supposed to do about this," while Libby was having her way with him.

Winnie humps his stuffed cow all the time. I accidentally locked this toy in a room and Winnie sat by the door for two days. When I figured out what was wrong, I unlocked the door and let him in. Winnie grabbed the cow, took it into the kitchen, humped it, took it into the den, humped it, then took it into the hallway where he continued to carry on. It took awhile before he finally collapsed.

Other Scorpios passions may take a different form.

Tiara, my holy terror Border Collie, finds people food very sensuous. Her idea of an orgy would be a weekend in the dumpster of Mama Gristanti's Restaurant.

When Thor wants his dad's attention, he'll share his lounge chair or roll over and present his belly; or look cute and needy; or bring his rawhide bone and dare Dad to take it. They fight on the floor a lot and it sounds seriously evil.

That last sentence, "sounds seriously evil," pretty much describes these sun signs. They might appear tough, but in reality they're sweethearts. Born in the middle months of fall, Scorpios are like kids dressed up for Halloween. They may look like ghosts and goblins, but under those scary masks are sensitive souls looking for sweetness in their big game of pretend.

The funniest incident happened at a local arts and crafts fair. Thor was on his leash, being admired and petted and loved by the people at the fair. Suddenly, he spotted another Dalmatian—actually a person collecting for the county Humane Society dressed in a Dalmatian suit. Instantly, Thor went wild lunging, snarling, snapping, and growling growls from hell. He was deeply offended when onlookers laughed so hard they cried.

Mink coats! My mother cannot wear her coat in my non-fur-home. The coat terrified Mandy. She acted as if she were afraid she might become a coat.

Although Uther scared me and many of those who came in contact with him, his owner loved him unconditionally.

Uther was a perfect 10! He was soulful, honest, brilliant, loyal, gorgeous, devoted, cautious, noble, gentle (with me), stoic, and courageous. Like a child, Uther responded to my moods. Whenever I was sad, he'd come around and let me burrow my sorrows in the scruff of his neck. He was the best companion a person could ever hope for in a canine. I was blessed to have had his friendship for nine years. I miss him terribly.

Ironically, so do I.

SAGITTARIUS
The Archer

 GOOD DOGGY:
adventurer
athletic
enthusiastic
friendly
generous
greeter
happy
spirited

BAD DOGGY:
careless
impatient
irresponsible
temperamental
stubborn

PAW PRINTS:

Shelby Bentley, Yorkshire Terrier
Jeep Craft, Dalmatian
Sam Horton, German Short-hair Pointer
Lexie McDermott, Rottweiller
Mollie Petersen, Schnauzer
Molly Stough, Brittany Spaniel
Hoover Tarrant, Golden Retriever

SAGITTARIUS
November 23–December 22
The Archer
I Understand

Jeep, my Dalmatian, literally prances when she walks. When Jeep gets
playful, she moves more like a horse than a dog. We figured it was
because she grew up around horses. Now, I know it's because she was
born under the half-horse, half-man sign of Sagittarius.

SAGITTARIUS is the ninth house in the zodiac and the last month of fall.
The crops planted in spring have now been harvested, and it's time to turn
one's thoughts to the cold and dormant months of winter. But not so fast!
Sagittarius is sandwiched between the two most pompous and serious-minded
sun signs. On one hand, we have Scorpio and its secretive ways, and on the
other we've got the sure-footed, serious Capricorn. If you think Sagittarius is
going to take its position lying down, think again. Sagittarians, with their element of Fire, are definitely going to light yours. These pups have no hidden
agendas. What you see is what you'll get. They will warm you with their sunny
dispositions and energize you with their exuberance. They'll put a smile on
your face as you watch their continuous celebration of life.

Sagittarius, symbolized by the Archer, the half-man, half-horse centaur,
represents both the physical and the intellectual spirit. Like the Archer,
Sagittarians can aim high and shoot straight, but they are easily sidetracked,
so don't be surprised if they gallop off in the opposite direction. As I said, this
sign celebrates life and they sure don't want to miss a minute of it.

Whereas Cancers do melodrama and Leos, Shakespeare, I see Sagittarians
as the stand-up comics of the zodiac who make eye contact with (or so it

seems) each and every member of their audience. As they strut their stuff back and forth across the stage, everyone feels a personal and intimate relationship with them and their performance. It's as if he or she is saying, "I see and love you! I see and love you! I see and love you!" If you know a Sagittarian, you know they have never met a stranger.

Unlike my Scorpio Uther, my Rottweiler Lexie was a precious, happy, playful doll baby. She was my four-legged angel who made everyone she met feel good. Every time someone came over, Lexie would turn herself inside out to greet them. She was constantly seeking me out for play and affection. She drove Uther up a wall. He spent his entire life trying to make her get serious.

Jeep is always wagging her tail, following you around trying to get closer to you. She just can't sit by you, she has to be sitting partly on you.

Sam loves everyone. He even tries to lick the fish when he's in our pond at the farm.

Molly, our Brittany Spaniel, is one friendly, sociable, enthusiastic animal. She has a vertical leap about five feet.

The Sagittarius motto is I UNDERSTAND, which means I understand what you're saying and feeling. This is one of Sagittarians' most endearing traits, because this sun sign really wants to please everyone. But because of their high energy levels, their enthusiasm sometimes gets in the way of reason, and they may not always come when called or do as you instruct.

Sagittarians are highly adaptable and can make the best of a bad situation.

They have a positive outlook on life and are the proverbial cockeyed optimists.

Those born under this sign are known for being the explorers . . . which is a nice way of saying these sun signs are nosey. Whereas an Aries is out to explore the world and Leos out to claim territory, Sagittarians just wanna have fun with whomever or whatever is around. They have a meet, greet, and move on attitude toward life.

Lexie was an incredible tracker. She had a bloodhound nose and sheer determination to accomplish a mission. She was a great pathfinder. If I asked her to do something, she'd look at me as if to say, "Leave a message. I'm too busy being distracted by all that's going on."

Jeep's very much into checking out new things. Even old things are searched in hopes of finding something new. If she loses or hides a toy, it will eventually be rediscovered . . . sometimes months later.

Mollie an explorer? Her nickname is Hunter Dog. She always has her nose to the ground on the trail of something or someone.

Sam loves our farm. His only difficulty is deciding what to investigate or visit next. Cats are fun, chickens are great, and horses are the living end! Sam goes in and out of places other dogs would never go. He puts his head into everything.

I own a cheese shop. If I take Hoover in after hours, he immediately starts searching for food. He'll stick his nose under a table that's maybe an inch off the floor and root. He finds the slightest of morsels.

Shelby gets relegated to the second floor when we have company. When everyone has left, he runs nose to the floor tracing their steps over and over again. It's very irritating.

In our yard, Hoover knows what time the deer appear and he will be on the lookout to woof them away.

As mentioned, Sagittarians are happy, generous, smart, and above all, enthusiastic. Their behavior can be described as excitable, and it doesn't take much to light their fire.

Lexie used to run at me doing 25 miles per hour, then she'd leap off the floor and tackle me to the ground. While I was down, she'd try to bury me as if I were a bone. Unbelievable high-strung energy.

Jeep is always on the move. She usually goes from front window to back window, inside then outside. Like there are so many things and she has to see and do everything at once. If I come home with anything (packages, bags, even mail), she has to see what it is. Visitors with purses are also a target.

High energy doesn't begin to describe Molly, our Brittany Spaniel. Many a guest has nearly been knocked senseless by her greetings.

Sam's like a ball of fire ready to explode. His body trembles with pent up energy. He doesn't wag his tail, he wags his entire body, and he gallops rather than runs. He's always on spin cycle.

Shelby, my Yorkie, is very positive and reacts to everything with vim and vigor. His litter mate, Mae Bee, literally twirls around on the floor while waiting to be picked up.

I named Hoover after the vacuum cleaner because he was always into everything—sucking it all up! He once inhaled an entire turkey.

Although curious, Sagittarians often have a hard time focusing on one thing at a time. In this respect, they have some of the same characteristics of Gemini.

Lexie flitted about like a butterfly and she'd often forgot to take seriously her duties as a guard dog. She'd rather have been distracted by play and making new friends.

Sam has a ten-second attention span and that's after I've spent ten minutes trying to divert him from the other fifty-seven things he's been looking for. Every part of his head acts as an antenna, and his neck reminds me of a periscope.

Shelby will see his reflection in something then frantically spend time trying to get it.

Sagittarians love to learn, please, and perform, but their high levels of energy and short attention spans can try your patience. There are pros and cons to obedience school. A class structure might restrict these free spirits as well as provide numerous diversions with all that's going on around them. Then again, being with others might give your dog the audience he loves, and he may perform beautifully. In short, they can go either way; be beauty or beast. As Molly's owner wrote, "What training? This animal has us trained." Then again, there's Jeep, whose participation in obedience school was very successful. Whatever you decide, remember to keep your pup focused. And applaud when they get something right.

Jeep watched what the other dogs did because she can't hear. We can't tell her things, but she knows hand signals and just seems to know what we want her to do.

Lexie's size made her tough to potty train. I just couldn't pick up a ninety pound pup and put her outside while she was in the midst of piddling. But she was a quick study and was housebroken within three days. However, she's never got the hang of walking on a leash or heeling. She had too much energy. She pushed ahead, crossing in front of me and tripping Uther.

Training Sam was difficult because of his high energy level and limited attention span. It's like Sam feels his energy through his skin. He has trouble staying still and is very vocal about needing my attention. He's also very stubborn. He disciplines easily but sometimes thinks "no" only applied to that last time he was told not to do something.

Calming your canines may not be easy. Catching them off guard is one way to temper the flames. When my sister's dog Mollie goes on a tear, she yells sit and her Schnauzer stops in mid-run. Other owners of Sagittarians resorted to taking them on a long run or having vigorous sessions of fetching a ball, while other owners simply used a firm voice and a glare of the evil eye.

If Shelby's tearing around the house or yard acting out-of-control, I'll holler belly rub, and immediately he stops what he's doing and flops on his back.

I have to pick up Sam and get him to make eye contact, which works for now. When he gets bigger, I'll have to hold his head in my hands and force him to look at me.

When Lexie got too rambunctious, I'd firmly state that is enough while making the time out gesture with my hands.

Punishing your Sagittarius might prove to be a guilt-producing effort because you'll probably feel awful eclipsing this happy-go-lucky sun sign.

If Jeep has done something wrong, she lets us know by cringing on the floor so we think she's been punished enough by guilt.

With Sam, harsh words or a raised voice devastates him. He hides behind me, drops his ears and tries to melt into the floor. It makes me feel like a witch.

Mollie does not take criticism well. Her ears go back, then she does the low crawl.

When Shelby's ashamed, his ears go back and his eyes get wide, then he runs off and hides.

And then there are Sagittarians who defy your admonishings.

When Hoover's caught rooting through the garbage, he'll hang his head although he still acts like he's done nothing wrong. It's as if he's telling me that I'm the one who's made the mistake. "Mom? Garbage? Me?"

Shelby is a slob. When reprimanded, he gives me a look that says, "Take me as I am or not at all."

Sagittarians tend to leap before they look, resulting in a lot of scrapes and scratches. It's not unusual to see this sun sign running into unopened doors or tripping on stairs. Like a child with a present, they're easily carried away by the moment. Seeing that they live in the moment, you should watch this fire sign more closely than the more grounded and down-to-earth signs like Taurus, Capricorn or Virgo.

If Sam is on to something—be it a kid or a butterfly—he forgets the bounds of acceptable behavior and nothing gets in his way.

During our wrestling matches, Lexie would lose herself and become Mad, Mad Max. She'd bark and yelp and dig into me with her front paws. She use to initiate these bouts by body slamming me. Even though she got wildly out of control, those moments were great fun.

Some sun signs are more talkative than others and Sagittarius is truly a Chatty Kathy.

Sam is always communicating. He has perfected a series of tonal whines, hums, and a sound that somewhat resembles an out-of-tune bag pipe running out of air. These are always accompanied by a head tilt, eye contact (with a person, object or playmate he's trying to reach), and an amazing array of ear positions. Placement of ears and height of pitch are in direct proportion to the urgency of his message.

When our elderly neighbor is working in her backyard, Jeep sits by the fence and talks to her. My neighbor talks right back, often explaining to Jeep what she's doing even though she knows Jeep is deaf.

Molly always talks to us. It's worth leaving home just for the greeting we get when we return.

In sum, The words to "You are my Sunshine" best describe Sagittarians. As Lexie's owner wrote:

Lexie was precious, feminine, sweet, beautiful, smart, happy, playful, spirited, delightful—another perfect 10. She was pure sweetness and made everyone she came in contact with feel good. Lexie was my angel dog, my bright four-legged angel.

CAPRICORN
The Goat

GOOD DOGGY:
authoritative
aspiring
cautious
disciplined
responsible
reserved
sure-footed

BAD DOGGY:
ambitious
egotistical
rigid
unforgiving
party pooper
calculating

PAW PRINTS:

Norman Hancock, Labrador Retriever
Sophie Hancock, Labrador Retriever
Bron Bernardi, Shetland Sheepdog
Lily Box, Golden Retriever
Shelby Bryan, Cocker Spaniel
Bark Early, Jack Russell Terrier
Willie Eicholtz, Cocker Spaniel
Peanut Fleck, Silky Terrier
Janna Petway, Standard Schnauzer
Brandy Runyon, Shih Tzu

Sweet Thompson, Lhasa Apso
Bambi Vassie, Pit Bull/Mix
Darcy Whelan, West Highland White Terrier

CAPRICORN

December 23–January 20

The Goat

I Use

And then there's my friend's pound puppy who hates hardwood floors. If his pup came running into an uncarpeted room, he'd find himself skidding across the floor. To avoid losing control, this clever canine now backs into such rooms.

"Sounds like a Capricorn to me," I said when told the dog was born around the end of the year. Capricorns are distinguished. They will do anything to avoid making fools of themselves. Now, if the dog had been a Sagittarius, he would have slid into a room like *Seinfeld*'s Kramer. If the dog were an Aquarian, he would have walked on hardwood because it was there!

Conservative. Cautious. Unemotional. Serious. Persistent. Dependable. Confident. Ambitious. Solitary? Well, meet CAPRICORN, the zodiac's version of Little Lord Fauntleroy. Capricorn is the tenth house on the astrological wheel. Symbolized by the GOAT, those born under this sign are able to cross difficult terrain with sure-footed ease. Capricorn's element is EARTH and, like Taurus and Virgo, Capricorns are grounded and down-to-earth. They have a no-nonsense attitude, so don't even think of messing with them.

CAPRICORN is the most determined sign in the zodiac, with an attitude as pompous and chilly as the winter months it ushers in.

Whereas Taurus doesn't like change and Virgo wants order, Capricorn craves routine. They are hard workers but only if they know what's expected of them. These sun signs aren't apt to jump into anything without first assessing the situation. In short, they don't want any part of surprise. Like Boy Scouts, they want to be prepared and abide by the rules, rules which are not meant to be broken.

Norman Schwarzkopf thinks and considers everything much like the general for whom he was named. He knows what he wants to do and when he wants to do it, which can be good or bad. But let there be no mistake when I say, he is not a dingbat!

Sister Sanctifying Sophie is a totally no-nonsense dog. Like a soldier with a plan, she thinks about everything and then decides what course to take. She may be busting her gut to do something, but she'll sit down and ponder a while before going for it, right or wrong. Her way means bombs away!

Brandy's every move is deliberate. Most of her time is spent planning what she'll do next. But, if I grab my car keys, she inevitably beats me out the door.

Bark Maverick reminds me of an athletic coach. He's very aggressive and bosses everyone around.

Jana never acts or reacts impulsively. You can see the wheels turning as she mulls over what action to take in any given situation. She's a thinker.

Peanut's always in charge and on patrol. She's not just the boss, she's the queen . . . and a royal pain in the ass. Peanut would make a great soldier. She literally polishes our leather furniture by spit-licking it.

I like to describe Capricorn as the 4-D Dog; dignified, detached, disciplined, and determined. You won't find this sun sign quick to gush over anyone or anything. That's not to say they aren't loving . . . they're just cautious and somewhat suspicious. Once a Capricorn gains your trust, he'll loyally love you for life. But don't expect him to paw all over you.

Contact with Peanut is on Peanut's terms, as is everything else. When she gets tired on a walk, she won't move, and I have to pick her up and carry her home. But, if I want to pick her up to pet her, forget it!

Brandy will greet someone only when she knows it's safe. She stays within eyesight but doesn't want physical contact.

Darcy doesn't like to be held or carried. She doesn't care to sit on my lap or in a chair with me for any length of time (maybe 30 seconds).

Bambi will let you pet her, but on her terms. If she's tired, don't touch. She will growl and show her teeth. She can't stand to be smothered.

If Sweetthing doesn't know a person, it's best they ignore him. He needs to decide when he's ready to say hi.

Jana wants to be with others but not necessarily touching them. Just being in the same room is enough.

Bron avoided much contact. He hated being groomed and he didn't like me scratching his stomach. He never rolled over to expose his tummy. I always wondered about that.

As mentioned, Capricorns have a no-nonsense attitude and like the Earth signs Taurus and Virgo, seem mature at birth. They are perfect examples of the term Old Goat. You won't find Capricorn exerting any frivolous behavior such as looking or acting foolish. (I know, I know . . . but the pound puppy mentioned at the start of this chapter has no idea how stupid he looks. He's just happy he's solved his problem.) Capricorns can make play seem like work, and fun and games a waste of time. Actually, the term wet blanket might also describe this sun sign. They sure can put a damper on things . . . literally . . . with their piss-on-it reactions.

When Peanut's mad, I expect a puddle. She'll use the garage or porch instead of the grass.

If I forget Shelby's in the basement, he'll pee on something to show his disapproval.

Although Brandy's a female, she lifts her leg to pee and constantly marks her territory outdoors.

Jana is a fun monitor. She allows only a specific amount of play between my other two dogs, then marches in and loudly announces that enough is enough. She abides by our rules without hesitation and believes it's her vocation in life to see that the rest of the dogs do so likewise.

Capricorn's motto is I USE which means they will use whatever's necessary to make their surroundings suitable to their needs. This sign is a control freak, a control freak with attitude. If something's not to their liking, they'll let you know! As a result, Capricorns can succeed in really getting your goat.

Norman thinks and responds to every situation accordingly. If he's left alone, he gets mad and figures out how he can get even with me—which results in his chewing up something.

When we got Darcy from the breeder, we were told she had a will and a way. Before she was six weeks old, she had already figured out how to get out of the kennel through the flap door. This didn't surprise the breeder as much as her learning how to get back in. When we got her home we put dividers across the doors out of our kitchen. The dividers were braced by hassocks and chairs. Very quickly, she figured out that if she jumped on to the hassock, she could scale the divider like a sure-footed goat.

Bron was not happy when we got a new puppy. When I came home and found a piece of chewed carpet, I thought it was the puppy, so I crated him when I went to work the next day. When I got home and found another piece of chewed carpet, I realized Bron was the culprit. He deliberately did it to get the puppy punished and out of his way. Another time Bron was warned not to get on the bed because I had a new comforter on it and was expecting guests. On a hunch, I drove the car to the front, then walked around the house to my bedroom window. There was Bron, sprawled out and completely at home, giving me that look.

Peanut literally runs the show at our house. She decides which dog's bowl to eat from—often it's all three. All toys are hers and she never lets the other two play with them.

When Willie got in a fight with my mother's dog, I called him on it. He sorta gave me the devil dog look and stalked out of the room.

Jana will act indifferent when she's annoyed by me. If she is annoyed by other dogs, she's quick to snarl.

Shelby has a corner of the couch that is his alone. If anyone sits there, including company, he will sit on top of them.

Capricorns should be easy to train because they want to be on the top rung of the proverbial ladder. They also hate to be rejected. You'll find these goats easily hoofing their way to the front of the class. However, if what they're doing doesn't seem to have a point or be of interest, they may balk. Don't act frivolous or act silly when teaching them manners. You might want to bark out the commands. Make like a drill sergeant, but don't scream your orders. Be firm. Let them know that training is a serious business. They'll respect you for it. Honest.

Bron loved going to obedience class. He didn't like the leash training at first, but soon realized it allowed him to could go places, and I never had anymore trouble.

Bambi was housebroken in less than two weeks. She learned how to push open the screen door to let herself out and pull it when she wants back in. She's never had any formal training but minds better than most children.

Without a doubt, Jana was easy to train. Her intelligence is sometimes frightening. Two or three repetitions and she has a new command down pat.

Brandy was easy to train. I never took her to obedience classes, but she goes along with the program.

Lily was the star of her obedience class!

Willie was very easy to train and seemed to learn new tricks on his own.

Capricorns don't like crowds. They will play just fine with other dogs, but they'd rather not be a part of the pack. This applies to human companionship as well. Unlike a Sagittarius who loves nothing better than to work a crowd, Capricorns prefer to be alone or in a one-on-one relationship. A Capricorn doesn't want to risk losing control of a crowd. If there are too many people or dogs around, this sun sign is apt to make himself scarce.

Bambi likes to sit on the front porch and watch people, but she hates a crowd.

Sweetthing tolerates being with a couple of people, but goes off when there's a crowd.

If there are too many people around, Jana retreats to her crate.

Darcy is very independent and would rather play by herself.

Now what does all of the above mean? Are we to take this sun sign as a cold, calculating canine? Not at all. Remember who was born on the 25th of December? A savior full of goodness and light; a man who sacrificed his life for the love of mankind; a man who healed the sick, fed the hungry, and forgave transgressions. Born under any sign of the Zodiac, dog spells love and goodness. When Capricorn loves, he loves unconditionally. Don't take his haughty disposition as uncaring, its just their nature. Go below Earth's surface. You'll see that Capricorn nurtures life and provides the bed for seeds to grow.

Capricorn: Conservative, cautious, sure-footed, dependable, confident?

Yes.

Calculating?

Perhaps.

Loved as much as any dog born under any of the astrological signs.

Most definitely.

BAMBI

Bambi has never failed to impress anyone who's met her. She loves her family and shows it daily. I kept my niece from six weeks to 1½ years. Bambi waited every morning at the door for her. She kissed her every day. She would drop her ball in her playpen to entertain her when she cried. Bambi would lay her head on the baby's lap while I fed her. She growled at me when the baby was wet so I knew to change her. When the baby began to walk, Bambi would quietly push her down when I told her not to go into a certain room.

Bambi can eat off a fork better than most kids. She also minds better than most kids.

Where I used to live, I had an above-ground pool. My friend brought her daughter over to swim. Bambi sat on the deck while her daughter got into the pool. When my friend stood up, so did Bambi. When my friend sat back down, Bambi came over to be petted. My friend could never get into the pool. She was puzzled by Bambi's behavior and figured out that she had yelled at her daughter in front of Bambi and Bambi was keeping them separated so my friend could not hurt her daughter.

Bambi climbed the pool ladder to make sure the kids in the pool were okay. She didn't understand that their screams were screams of fun.

My mom passed away a few years ago. My niece had just turned two. We were at my house for Thanksgiving and my niece was leaving and kissing everyone goodbye. She kissed her Nana, then me. She put both hands on Bambi's face and kissed her on the mouth. My mom died knowing Bambi would never hurt my niece, her grandchild.

BRON

Bron's been gone for a few years now, but I still cry a little every day, usually in the morning or evening before going to sleep. He was my life nearly every day for 15 years. I'd spent more time with Bron than I had with my own parents.

White Castle hamburgers were his favorite treat, and every month or so, he'd get four. He loved them, buns, onions, hamburgers, pickles. He never got sick, but near the end, he did burp a few times after eating them. I never fed him much in the way of people food, but White Castles were a special treat and he knew it. He also knew the name. I had his picture taken and wanted him to look alert, so I told the photographer to say White Castles. He did and got a great shot. I bought him a dozen for *his last meal, and I've never eaten one since. Just driving by one makes me cry.*

For over 15 years, Bron was my closest companion. If I had one wish, it would be that Bron were human because we were soul mates. I've always had dogs in my life, including my first who lived over seventeen years, but Bron has set a high standard, and, for the first time, I'm not sure if I will ever want another. There will never be another Bron.

Filling out this survey brought back those special moments, and it was an emotional experience, but I don't mind too much because he was a special dog and well worth it. I'm proud to tell his story.

AQUARIUS
The Water Bearer

 GOOD DOGGY:
curious
friendly
independent
intellectual
inventive
spirited
willful

BAD DOGGY:
detached
eccentric
unpredictable
rebellious
scattered
temperamental

PAW PRINTS:

P.J. San Angelo, Miniature Schnauzer
Ruby Bartholomew, Vizsla
Olive Cooper, Boston Terrier
Einstein Fleck, Bichon Frisé
Dewey Harris, Shih Tzu
Beamer Jenkins, Standard Poodle
Tipyn Johnson, Welsh Corgi
Oppie Pike, Standard Poodle
Ike Swope, German Shepherd

AQUARIUS
January 21—February 18
The Water Bearer
I Know

My dentist was telling me about his new puppy. He's the same breed as the one we've had for five years, but their personalities are completely different.

"When was he born," I asked.

"January or February," he said.

"Is your puppy grounded and down to earth or does he have a will of his own?"

"Oh, gawd," he replied rolling his eyes, "a will of his own!"

"Well, let the sunshine in. You own an Aquarius," I said laughing.

AQUARIUS is the eleventh house in the zodiac. Because it's symbolized by THE WATER BEARER, one would assume that Aquarius would have water as its element, but one's assumption wouldn't hold water . . . so pour that logic down the drain. Aquarius, the Water Bearer's ELEMENT is AIR. Is this not a contradiction in terms? That's because Aquarius is our paradoxical pooch who can blow any which way. Whereas Scorpio is the most mysterious of sun signs, Aquarius is the most individualistic. The one thing Aquarians have in common is that they're all different. Unpredictable and eccentric, there is no such thing as average when describing this sun sign. Owning an Aquarius is like flying a kite—your judgement and control are at the mercy of the winds.

Aquarius is the zodiac's eccentric free spirit, the rugged individualist who's been described as the humanitarian of the zodiac. Saint or sinner? You decide. Although not a dual sign, these pups can be an enigma. Aquarians can be shy and introverted or larger than life. Some are friendly and loyal, others unemotional and aloof. They will do anything for you unless something better comes along. They can be impatient and independent to the point of wanting to be left alone. Then again, Aquarians can't stand being left out of anything. They want to know what's going on at all times. They can be flighty or focused.

Confused?

Let's make this easy. As my mother used to say, all dogs that are out, want in, and all dogs that are in, want out. Seeing that we own no bad dogs, let's treat this sun sign as puppies and concentrate on their lighter, less complex side. In doing so, you'll find these highly energized mass of contradictions truly a breath of fresh air. Aquarians can't help it if they're flighty or spaced out. It's not their fault, it's their element.

Beemer will run into things because he doesn't pay attention. He's always tripping on the porch steps trying to watch the dogs next door.

Ike has a very short attention span. He's easily distracted, especially by noise.

Dewey will play with a toy for only a short time before running off to do something else.

I don't have any problem with Einstein's attention span. He has none. I never know what he's going to do next.

P.J.'s attention span is very short. She'll obey some commands only until she gets her treat. Stay is a very difficult word for her to understand.

Sometimes when we call Olive to come, she just gives us this blank stare. If she's chasing a ball, she'll stop and wander off as if she's totally forgotten what she was doing.

Now on the other hand, you might find your Aquarian so focused that his vision can't be blurred. Ike's owner writes:

"Although most of the time Ike has no attention span, he sometimes will take all his toys, place them in a perfect line, and study them for quite some time."

Aquarians' attention span, short or long, may make them look like nit wits, but don't be fooled by appearance. In reality, Aquarians are smart, inventive, and curious. In fact, their motto, I KNOW, means I know that! Why? Because Aquarians, with their inquiring minds, need to know. They are always checking things out, seeing who's at the door or who's walking down the street because they're nosey. Problem is, they don't give themselves enough time to get the complete picture and often miss the facts. Why? Because something else is occurring—over there! Einstein's owner, for instance, has to warn anyone who comes over to keep an eye on their possessions.

Einstein is a real sneak. He'll take things from purses and pockets. By the time I catch him, whatever he's found has been destroyed. He's positively into everything.

With Aquarians, what you see is what you get . . . if you can pin them down for any length of time. Aquarians have no hidden agenda because they have no agenda. They just do their own thing or have you do it for them.

I have to lift Beemer into the car or onto my bed, if he wants up. But he'll easily clear the four-foot hedge in the backyard if he wants to play with the neighbor's dogs.

Aquarians go for the sake of going. They walk the walk and talk the talk—they're the humanitarians of the zodiac. If they'd slow down, they could save the world . . . maybe. If they just didn't have to take such a circuitous route! But, alas, you'll never see an Aquarius travel in a specific direction as would a predictable earth sign such as Capricorn.

Olive never stops. Walk in the door and she'll have your shoelaces untied before you've crossed the threshold. Then she'll race from room to room, catapulting onto counter tops to see what's on them. An electric fence makes it easier to let her outside without her running away (her former modus operandi). When she wants to play, she's still relentless. It's hard to settle her down.

When Ruby gets excited, she runs figure eights through the house even up and over our furniture. She loves to ride in the car but isn't interested once we reach our destination. She just loves to go!

Ruby usually gets very excited when I come home. However, every now and then she doesn't acknowledge my entering the door. And sometimes she acts as if she's done something wrong when, in fact, she hasn't.

In addition to being entertaining and independent, Aquarians can be stubborn. Like Libra, this sun sign tends to have an it's-my-way-or-the- highway outlook on life. As an owner, you will have to make things challenging to get and keep your pups' interest. If you don't, they'll be off on their next adventure or trying your patience. Remember, these are free spirits.

> *If I don't make things challenging enough for Ike, he'll take off on a head trip. Although physically with me, he appears to be somewhere else entirely. Its like he's riding another wave length.*

> *The only time Olive's focused is when she's digging holes. Other than that, I can't figure out what she wants.*

> *If Ike doesn't like my approach to a new lesson (say picking a bunch of keys off the floor) he'll simply let out a moan, paw at the keys, and lie down.*

> *Oppenheimer will come at a snail's pace when he doesn't want to do something, like come when called. However, when Oppy's accosted by an aggressive dog, he takes it as a joke and runs circles around the offender, taunting him/her to catch him. It really annoys the other dog.*

All of the above means that training Aquarians can be a challenge. A strong, firm voice and eye contact will help with focus. Physical exercise before a learning session will help rid them of some of their energy, although a simple praise or a treat might work just as well. Aquarians hate rejection, so they probably won't want to repeat any mistakes made in an obedience class. Then again, all the other dogs might be too much of a distraction for them. Repetition might bore them into obeying. Then again, it might not. You know your dog best. You'll figure out what course to take.

Ruby is extremely headstrong. If I'm leaving, she'll bolt out the door, lie down on the lawn, roll over, and refuse to budge. Yelling at her does nothing. It's as if she has me trained. I have to go to her, get down on the ground, rub her tummy, and tell her how wonderful she is before I can coax her back into the house. It takes awhile, but it works.

Rules? Dewey has a hard time playing by them. He knows not to chew the window ledge, but he does it anyway. He does remember getting spanked but goes on and does what he wants to . . . he will not take no for an answer, and he continues to nip at me despite constant smacks on his nose. But, he's a cutie, so he often gets his way.

I was ready to send Tipyn back during training. She was so difficult I had to put her in the down position for 30 minutes twice a day for several months until she learned that I was in charge and she had to listen!

Tipyn's owner was lucky to keep her Aquarian down for longer than a few seconds! As Ike's mom writes, "If I leave him in a down-stay, he has a hard time coping."

Some owners bag obedience school after the second session. Beemer's owner writes:

At home, he heels on lead and sits off lead or down stays, but in class I had to drag him through the commands. On stand stays, he'd tuck his tail and hang his head as if I had beaten him! Everyone in the class thought it was a riot . . . everyone but me. He was the only dog who refused to learn a weekly trick. It was so embarrassing!

Aquarians are very in tune with human emotions and seem to sense if someone's worried or sad, even if the person's not aware of it himself. Often Aquarians have the ability to second guess their owners.

> *Ike's the first telepathic dog I've lived with. I can mentally be planning to go for a walk and there's Ike standing in front of me as if to say, "Well, what are you waiting for, let's go!"*

> *Even before I make a move or speak a word, Oppy knows when we're going for a walk. He can be outside or completely out of my sight, but he knows. If I put walking shoes on indoors and he's outside, he's on the other side of the door barking.*

Being independent and off in all directions, this sun sign might be perceived as being detached and aloof. Au contraire. Aquarians are very loyal, and once they decide someone's okay, they become devoted. Although very independent, Aquarians need to be loved as much as any dog. However, you might have to wait until the winds calm and the air is stilled before this love child doles out his affections. Aquarians would rather make love than war, but one never knows when they're going to board the next peace train. That's not to say YOU can't be affectionate at any and all times toward them.

> *Does Beemer want everyone to love him? Yes! Yes! Yes! If someone ignores him, he keeps returning to them until he will makes that person want him.*

> *Dewey constantly licks me on the face, especially around my mouth and ears. He finds it hard to wait his turn if I am petting our other dog. But once Dewey gets his turn, he's off.*

Ruby thinks everyone she likes wants her in their lap. If ignored, she will sulk and act depressed. Her head and ears droop and she'll walk away. It's really a pitiful sight to see.

Ike loves everyone once he gets to know them.

P.J. believes she's the center of the universe.

When Aquarians want something, they are relentless. Ignoring them is a lesson in futility as is telling them to lighten up. Take food, for example. If you happen to be munching on something an Aquarius wants, Aquarius will do everything to see that Aquarius gets . . .

We try to hold out feeding Olive table scraps but there's all that staring and whining. She'll climb up on the back of an armchair so she's eye level with us while we eat.

Beemer will grab food off the table if he's not put in a down-stay.

Dewey doesn't stare, he simply helps himself. Once I was eating a cream-filled wafer, and he unexpectedly jumped up and bit off the end that wasn't in my mouth.

Ruby sits perfectly still and erect. Only her eyes move from my fork to my mouth while she looks as if she's starving.

Einstein dances on his hind legs and whines and barks for a treat. Scolding him falls on deaf ears. He just looks at me, then runs to the dog treat cabinet and barks for a reward. He has no clue that he's done any-thing wrong.

So what do you do with these feisty, happy-go-lucky, artful dodging, free spirits with a will of their own? Give them freedom under acceptable limitations. Teach them new tricks and games. Find new places to explore. Engage in plenty of physical activity, but don't count on any long-range planning. Unlike Capricorns, Aquarians believe that rules can be bent if not broken. If rules get in their way, ignore! If your Aquarius is like Beemer, who's never submitted to an angry person or dog—even when corrected—then you'll just have to live with it. Let down your hair and let this sun sign's sun shine through. After all, this now is The Age of Aquarius, so make like a beautiful balloon and fly up-up-and-away. You just might learn to love their feeling of freedom and revel in never knowing what to expect.

PISCES
The Fishes

 GOOD DOGGY:
compassionate
emotional
intuitive
kind
quiet
reserved
sensitive
sympathetic

BAD DOGGY:
apathetic
careless
confused
melancholy
timid
vague
wimp

PAW PRINTS:
Melody Austin, Bernese Mountain Dog
Abby Casey, Labrador Retriever
Jubie Cavett, Boxer
 Rip Cheski, Golden Retriever
Heidi End, Miniature Schnauzer
Bear Fangman, Labrador Retriever
Zoe Hart, Golden Retriever
Sam Johnson, Labrador Retriever
Gromit Lundy, Australian Shepherd

Isabelle O'Neil, Border Collie/Mix
Spotts Roland, Cocker/Pit Bull Mix
Spirit Schultz, Golden Retriever

PISCES
February 19–March 20
The Fish
I Believe

Sam, our fox-red Labrador, is extremely sensitive and intuitive. He knows when we're happy, when were sad, angry, etc. He tends to mirror our feelings and shows this with his body language. He knows when I'm coming home, even when my car is several blocks away—he'll get up and go to the door in anticipation of my arrival.

Sam's birthday is March 8, which makes him a Pisces.

PISCES, the twelfth and final house in the zodiac, brings the astrological wheel full circle. Pisces is often seen as moving away from the physical into the spiritual world. Whereas Aries is the first month of spring and represents beginnings, Pisces is the last month of winter and represents endings. Pisces has traveled through all the houses to reach its destination, absorbing, along the way, many of their attributes. With Pisces, you might experience the determination of Aries, the stubbornness of Taurus, the flightiness of Gemini, the emotions of Cancer, the kingliness of Leo, Virgo's love of order, Libra's need for balance, Scorpio's sting, the enthusiasm of Sagittarius, Capricorn's desire to achieve, or an Aquarian's need to know.

Pisces is the last of the three signs whose element is WATER. In astrology, water represents the emotions. Whereas Cancers' feelings are open and out front, and Scorpios' are secreted beneath the surface, the waters of Pisces reflect that which surrounds them. Pisces is the chameleon of the zodiac and can blend into any situation. Pisces may be sunny when skies are clear, may darken when storms move in, seem on fire beneath the setting sun, or be cold and aloof when the air is chilled.

Water signs can also be compared to their season. The waters of Cancer nurture the growth of summer while the waters of Scorpio chill in autumn's air. Pisces' waters, although reflective, can also become foggy as winter warms into spring, making this sign often difficult to comprehend. You know something's going on, but you just can't see, feel, or touch its essence.

In astrology, water isn't normally viewed as a destructive force. In fact, water signs hate conflict and will find a way to avoid uncomfortable situations. Cancers can bury themselves, pull into their shells or side step whatever's in their way. Scorpios might sting the troublesome source, while Pisces might opt to swim off in the opposite direction. But remember, although water signs may appear meek, their element can take different shapes. Water can make its way over, under, around, or through whatever is in their way. In other words, water wimps can also be water warriors.

Pisces is the second dual sign, the first being Gemini. Pisces' icon is a FISH with two heads pointed in opposite directions. Pisces live in a world of feelings and want to take the path of least resistance. It's easier for this sun sign to go with the flow, ride along on the emotions of others, and, to quote Shakespeare, "Aye, there's the rub!"

Pisces' reactions relate and equate to the influences around them. Those born with the element of air can blow in all directions, those with fire are energized, and those with the element of earth are grounded. Pisces' path is a watered-down two-way street.

If you, as owner, are an Aries, your Pisces pooch might be adventuresome. If you're an egotistical Leo or a justice-seeking Libra, your Pisces might reflect your sense of kingliness or justice.

Another difference which surfaces within the three water signs has to do with survival. Cancer Crabs and Scorpio Scorpions can live in or out of water. Pisces The Fish cannot.

Ever heard the phrase "out of ones element," or "he's like a fish out of water?" Well, the phrases are reasoned and true. Pisces' perspective is limited to what's beneath the surface. Submerged and apart from the real world, the Pisces personality becomes vague and harder to fathom than their crustacean and arachnid cousins. Again, our understanding of Pisces becomes limited. What's really going on we might never know.

There are definitions which can be applied to this sun sign. Pisces like strong personalities. They are loyal and doggedly devoted to those they love. Their motto, I BELIEVE, translates into I BELIEVE I AM HERE TO SERVE.

When Sam was about seven months old, I sank to the bottom of the pool just for fun. Sam, thinking I was in trouble, immediately came to my rescue. He grabbed my hand and pulled me to the surface.

Another time, my wife was caught in a bad rainstorm with Sam. He immediately headed for home, but would stop and wait at strategic points to make sure she was coming and was okay.

Gromit leaps to his feet, even from a nap, when one of his people gets up to go anywhere. While we all eat in the kitchen, he circles the table to make sure we are secure. He's very protective.

Gus feels as if he must protect me from vicious big animals such as horses and deer.

Jubie is a very good watch-pet. She guards her house, me, and my van.

Spirit is definitely a guard dog. If I could give him a title, it would be Professional Greeter, but after he's given someone a lick and a paw, it's like "Now what can I do for you?"

Now there's that flip side of Pisces, the side that says: YOU ARE HERE TO SERVE ME. As you know, Leo is the King of the Jungle and expects to be waited on at all times! Although not as pronounced, Pisces prefer the same treatment.

Abby's motto is more like "You're here to serve me." She seems to believe I was born just to play with her.

Maymie believes she's the most important member of the household and is the one in charge. It's everyone's job to satisfy her, and she doesn't let us forget it for one moment.

With their ability to reflect and absorb, Pisces will literally feel your pain. If you're happy, your Pisces will be happy. If you're moping around, your dog will mope around too. So if your dog sighs deeply and seems to have a hard time overcoming inertia, you might try some personal soul searching. Understand thyself and you shall understand your pet Pisces.

Gromit is very good at sensing sadness in his humans and offering unob-trusive comfort.

If I come home from work and I don't feel like taking Isabelle for a walk, she can tell and doesn't push it. She puts her head in my lap when I am sad.

Jubie's sad when I'm sad, and happy when I'm happy. She knows my moods.

Abbey's very sensitive, but she seems to get more agitated if I scold her. She responds better when she thinks she's hurt me. I get her attention by pouting.

Heidi seems to know what I'm going to do before I do. We're both very keyed into each other.

As mentioned, water signs are neither confrontational nor competitive. Unlike the Crab who will bury itself from any unpleasantness, Pisces' main defense is to swim in the opposite direction. Pisces can display a temper, but are more likely to cop out before they act out. They'd rather take the path of least resistance and go with the flow.

Sam is easily excitable but he never displays a temper. He has a very sweet disposition. He's friendly to people and submissive to other dogs.

Gromit does bark at people walking down the street or when he hears a noise, but once the door is open, he's very friendly. In the park he goes out of his way to avoid macho dogs.

When my daughter's dog visited for a couple of weeks, Gus smoldered. When his grumbling growls erupted, there was sound and fury but no pain inflicted.

If you fuss at Spotts at all, he acts as if his heart is breaking. I'm glad to report that he is a very good dog and doesn't get scolded much. When he is bad, he usually tells on himself via his demeanor.

My older dog intimidates Isabelle. She always gives Isabelle a mean look and a thorough sniff when she gets back from Agility classes on Saturdays. Isabelle stands still, avoids eye contact, and always tinkles on the floor.

Jubilee has very, very little temper. Doesn't like confrontation at all, and does take the path of least resistance.

Although not confrontational, Pisces is impatient and will often seem restless. My friend's dog, Bud, will bark steadily when he's ready to go for a walk. He'll also bark his steady bark if she stops and talks to someone. Sam will do the same.

Sam is very demanding and will bark until we do what he wants. But if his wants conflict with ours, he is quick to do what we want him to do.

Spirit is always looking for something to do. He bores easily. If we don't do our two-hour woods romp everyday, he gets into some trouble at home; chewing, for example, on things he shouldn't be chewing.

Gromit paces often, especially in the evening when the family is together watching TV. But, he's a great travel dog, and will ride contentedly for hours in the back seat. He's always ready to get in the car.

Spotts likes to play with other dogs, but is also ready to go home with me at the end of play session. He tells me when she's had enough.

Melody, my Bernese Mountain Dog, is highly excitable—goes everywhere on the run—reminds me of Kramer on Seinfeld *when she comes into a room.*

The only thing that excites Maymie are snacks. At night, she sits on my side of the couch until about nine. Then she moves next to my husband because she knows that about that time he gets his own snack. If she hears him open the pantry, she perks up and listens. If he opens a fruit pie box or Cheetos bag, she runs to the kitchen and does little flips all the way back to the den because she knows she'll get a piece. It's the same with ice cream because she gets to lick the bowl. If he doesn't give her her share fast enough, Maymie will let out a small whine every few seconds.

Aside from being loyal, sensitive, intuitive, and restless, Pisces sometimes has a hard time making a decision. Even if a choice is made, senior moments are apt to set in, and they'll forget what it was they decided. If your Pisces seems missing, he might just be off in search of that pot of gold! After all, a rainbow's glow is created by drops of reflected water.

Pisces can also be impulsive and can repeatedly make the same mistakes because they often have a hard time getting it. Remember, all dogs that are in shall want out, and all dogs that are out shall want in. As with air-headed Gemini, you need to get your water-logged Pisces focused. Be firm and direct in conveying what you want from them.

Sometimes we'll throw a ball for Sam and for a second he'll debate with himself, should I chase it or should I not?

Abbey will swim into lakes and rivers to catch ducks, which are smart enough to stay just beyond her reach. No matter how long or how hard I call, she won't come until she's on the verge of exhaustion. I think it goes back to her retrieving a very dead 10-pound fish a few years ago. She thinks that if she can catch a fish, albeit dead, then she can catch a duck!

Gromit's indecisive, especially if he needs to go out when we're inside. He likes to have me open the door and then will stand there contemplating his choices.

Bear, nicknamed Jaws because he loves to chew, looks so ashamed when scolded. However, he returns to his inappropriate behavior when he thinks no one is looking. Bear is constantly visiting neighbors, then promptly forgets how to get back home.

Spirit gets restless. Sometimes when we settle in at night, he curls up on the floor, looks at me, and moans. It's as if he isn't sure what he wants.

Zoe will go out in the yard and just look around, like she's thinking "What shall I do first." Sometimes when I open the door for her to come in, she just stands and stares at me.

Many astrologers see Pisces as the champion of the underdog. Pisces' ability to connect with all the houses in the astrological wheel make them our universal social workers. Dogs born under this sign should be good as seeing-eye dogs or those involved in the areas of search and rescue. Pisces work well with others because they don't need to be number one. Of course, this might not be the case if their owner is an Aries, or the dog's birth date is close to

Aries. If possible, you might want to involve your dog in some cause as has Spirit's owner who writes:

> *I'm outgoing, friendly, and fun-loving, just like Spirit. I wanted a dog that had some jobs. One of Spirit's is he's my companion hiking buddy. He also does volunteer work with me. We visit nursing homes, and he goes with me to schools where I give motivational talks to students. He wears a green backpack stuffed with gifts I give to them. I call him Spirit, the self-esteem sniffing dog.*

Or Rip's owner who writes:

> *Rip is the most loving, responsive pet I've ever had. He understands and loves his job, which is being a trained show dog.*

Living in a world of water, Pisces have the power to create that which they cannot see. Many actors, writers, composers, and musicians are born under this sign. If not a cause, give Pisces a part to play or a routine to follow. Spott's owners, for example, encourage his nightly patrol of the yard and reward his efforts with praise. After all, what this sign needs most is confidence. Sometimes this just means giving them time to be alone.

> *Rip likes to go out on the deck every night and sit and meditate for about 20 minutes. He's not ready for bed until he does, and he gets very agitated if he doesn't have his time alone.*

As emphasized, Pisces like to serve and will wait on your table for more than just scraps. But remember, Pisces need to get something in return. Show your appreciation, applaud their actions, and send them positive vibes. You might not get them out of the water, but you sure can pull them toward the surface to tread water for awhile. You won't get them out of their milieu but you might, just might, get a clearer and closer look at that gem you're fortunate enough to call your own.

SUNSPOT SURVEYS

The following questions appeared on the "Sun Spot" questionnaires. If you are unsure of your dog's sign, you may consider these surveys to find clues.

ARIES
March 21—April 20

Aries is the first sign in the Zodiac. Does your dog want to be number one?

Is your dog impatient?

Is your dog a battering ram or gentle as a lamb?

Would you describe your dog as energized?

Does your dog like to learn?

Can your dog be described as determined?

Is your dog prone to accidents?

Would you describe your dog as arrogant?

Does positive reinforcement work better than yelling at your pet?

Does your dog have any hang-ups?

If your dog were to describe itself, how would (s)he complete the phrase

"I am"?

TAURUS
April 21—May 21

Does your dog hate change?

Could your dog could be described as passive and patient?

As a puppy, did your dog need a lot of food?

Does your dog have a hard time overcoming inertia?

Would you describe your dog as dependable?

Can your dog be very stubborn?

Does your pet loves to be cuddled and hugged?

Is your dog is a loyal and devoted companion?

Does your dog have a great deal of strength and endurance?

Does your dog have any hang-ups?

If your dog were to describe itself, how would (s)he complete the phrase

"I have"?

GEMINI
May 22—June 21

Do references to air, such as airhead and spacecadet, help to describe your
  dog?

Does your dog seem to have more than one personality?

Is your dog cheerful and playful, the perpetual child?

Is your dog easily bored?

Does your dog come up with quick solutions?

Would you describe your pet as inventive?

Is your dog a great ham who loves to perform?

Does your dog just love everyone?

Does your dog have a hard time making choices?

Does your dog have any hang-ups?

If your dog were to describe itself, how would (s)he complete the phrase
  "I think"?

CANCER
June 22—July 22

Is your dog is timid, sensitive, and intuitive?

Do conflicts make your dog nervous?

Does your dog have separation anxieties and tend to follow you from room to room?

Would your dog rather be inside than out, unless you are outside?

Does your dog hate loud noises?

Was your dog easy to train?

Is your dog melodramatic, especially when you come home?

Does your dog love stuffed animals and is he or she gentle with them?

Is your dog a good escape artist?

Does your dog have any hang-ups?

If your dog were to describe itself, how would (s)he complete the phrase "I feel"?

LEO
July 23—August 23

Does your dog act as if (s)he were king of the jungle?

Does your dog seem very proud of itself?

If your dog were an actor, what role would (s)he play?

Is your dog territorial?

Is your dog inquisitive or downright nosey?

Does your dog often act aloof?

Is your dog protective of you?

Does your dog get rambunctious?

Does your dog like to be groomed?

Does your dog have any hang-ups?

If your dog were to describe itself, how would (s)he complete the phrase

"I will"?

VIRGO
August 24—September 22

Is your dog high-strung, and expect things to go their way?

When things don't go their way, do they let you know?

Is your dog reliable and dependable?

Will your dog balk when (s)he is not sure what you expect?

Your dog does not be like being the center of attention, right?

Is your dog very picky and apt to smell a treat before accepting it?

Does your dog prefer order and routine?

Does your dog have a great grasp of language?

Does your dog love to be pampered and groomed?

Does your dog have any hang-ups?

If your dog were to describe itself, how would (s)he complete the phrase

"I analyze"?

LIBRA
September 23—October 23

Is your dog balanced or unbalanced?

Does your dog do better with order or disorder?

Is your dog really into pleasing you?

Does your dog ever act spacey?

Is your dog a charming social butterfly?

Does your dog have mood swings?

Would your dog rather cooperate or compete?

Does your dog need a lot of affection?

How does your dog feel about being left alone?

Does your dog have any hang-ups?

If your dog were to describe itself, how would (s)he complete the phrase

"I balance"?

SCORPIO
October 24—November 22

Would you describe your dog as sneaky?

Does your dog have a large ego?

Is your dog very protective or on a power play with you?

Would you describe your dog as intense?

Does (s)he need a lot of exercise?

Would you consider your dog sensual?

Does your dog remember every kindness and every injustice?

Scorpio is a water sign. What kind of water form best describes your dog?

　　(Babbling brook, tidal wave, snow, sleet, rain, etc.)

Does your dog share it's toys?

Does your dog have any hang-ups?

If your dog were to describe itself, how would (s)he complete the phrase

　　"I desire"?

SAGITTARIUS
November 23—December 22

Does your dog have a sunny, cheerful, perhaps exaggerated, disposition?

Would you describe your dog as a whirling dervish?

Was your dog into everything the moment (s)he first squirmed out of your arms?

Does your dog know how to "work a crowd"?

Would your dog make an average, good, or great explorer?

Does your dog have a short attention span?

How does your dog react if scolded?

What's your best method for calming your dog?

Was your dog easy or hard to train?

Does your dog have any hang-ups?

If your dog were to describe itself, how would (s)he complete the phrase "I understand"?

CAPRICORN
December 23—January 20

Does your dog have a down-to-earth, no-nonsense personality?

Does your dog jump into situations or assess them first?

Is your dog self-assured?

Would your dog prefer to be alone or with others?

Do you often want to tell your dog to "lighten-up"?

Would you describe your dog as aloof?

How does your dog respond to physical contact? Is (s)he a touchy-feely sort of pet?

Was your dog easy to train?

Is your dog competitive with other dogs?

Does your dog have any hang-ups?

If your dog were to describe itself, how would (s)he complete the phrase "I use"?

AQUARIUS
January 21—February 18

Does your dog have a hard time following rules?

Does your dog have a short attention span.

Is your dog stubborn/head strong?

Does your dog crave approval and acceptance?

Do your dog's actions often surprise you?

Is your dog intelligent?

Would you refer to your dog as a free spirit?

How does your dog relate to other animals?

Does you dog ever act like the proverbial dumb blond?

Does your dog have any hang-ups?

If your dog were to describe itself, how would (s)he complete the phrase

"I know"?

PISCES
February 19—March 20

Could your dog's motto be "Here to Serve"?

Is your dog overly sensitive?

Does your dog seem to reflect your moods?

Is your dog indecisive?

Is your dog often restless?

Is your dog often indecisive?

Would your dog prefer to do nothing or have a specific job?

At times, does your dog seem to have more than one personality?

How does your dog adapt to new situations?

Does your dog have any hang-ups?

If your dog were to describe itself, how would (s)he complete the phrase

"I believe"?